A Century of Images

THE GIBSON SHOP IN PENZANCE, *c.* 1880

A CENTURY OF IMAGES

PHOTOGRAPHS BY THE GIBSON FAMILY

REX COWAN
IN COLLABORATION WITH
FRANK GIBSON

INTRODUCTION BY
JOHN LE CARRÉ

ANDRE
DEUTSCH

First published in 1997 by André Deutsch Limited
A subsidiary of VCI plc
106 Great Russell Street, London WC1B 3LJ

A CIP record for this book is available from
the British Library
ISBN 0 233 98992 7

Design by the Senate
Printed by Caledonian International Book Manufacturing Ltd, Glasgow

CONTENTS

ACKNOWLEDGEMENTS

My thanks foremost to Zélide Cowan, who first fully appreciated the importance of the Gibson collection of photographs, and whose compendious knowledge of the genealogy of the Isles of Scilly helped to fill in hitherto unpublished details of the family. Janette Rozing, whose collecting of Gibson photographs is dedicated and relentless, supplied several prints that have long been lost and that now embellish this book. Dr Eric Richards of Penzance generously steered me through the identification and dating of several of the images from his extensive knowledge and library. And Clive Mumford, editor of *The Scillonian*, helpfully gave permission for the publication in my text of extracts from past issues.

Rex Cowan

DESPITE MODERN NAVIGATIONAL AIDS, SHIPS WILL ALWAYS BE SNARED ON SCILLY.
FRANK GIBSON WAS THERE TO PHOTOGRAPH THE ANTIGUA-REGISTERED CONTAINER SHIP *CITA* WHEN ON 26 MARCH 1997
SHE STRUCK A REEF OFF ST MARY'S, NEAR THE SPOT WHERE SIR CLOUDESLEY SHOVELL'S BODY WAS REPUTEDLY WASHED UP IN 1707.

THE INHERITOR
JOHN LE CARRÉ

'I never thought of taking up any other profession,' says Frank Gibson, and gives a surprising, high-pitched giggle that seems to belong to somebody else.

But Frank isn't talking about his love of photography. He is talking about doing what he is told. 'We were two brothers. I was the elder boy, so I came into the business and my brother went on to Oxford to study because he was bright and had an aptitude for languages. He eventually got himself into Lloyd's International.'

So was he happy? I ask, knowing by now that Frank prefers to talk of others rather than himself.

Frank's face closes like a door, which it can do at any time. Probably he was happy with his work, he concedes, while his shrug begs the question of whether anybody who was tied to a desk could be in touch with happiness.

But there is good news too. His brother has now retired to Cornwall. Redemption is at hand.

We are on the island of St. Mary's, where Frank lives and has his photographic business. Scilly comprises five inhabited islands and some hundred-odd islets, and lies twenty-eight miles south-west of Land's End. St. Mary's, two-and-a-half miles across and nine miles of coastline, is the largest and, with around 1,600 residents, the most densely populated and overbuilt.

Frank is a brittle, complex man, spirited and twinkly but reserved. Like most people who live close to nature, he is a bit of an authoritarian, a bit secretive, a bit deep. He is good at greeting you and quick to size you up. But sustaining a conversation with him, particularly if it touches upon matters close to his personal life, is something of a game. Unwelcome questions are greeted with a gust of laughter – but when the laughter ends you discover that you have moved on to a different subject.

He is in his mid-sixties, spare, homy and agile. You can see that he takes care of himself. You feel he keeps himself in check. When he was younger, that couldn't have been so easy. He loves Scilly with all his heart. There's Scilly and there's the rest of the world. Its beauty is a religion to him, its desecration – the overbuilding of St. Mary's, the people-pollution that results when mass tourism replaces traditional culture – is a personal agony.

Eight years back he resigned in anger from a leading position on the Board of Trustees of the Isles of Scilly Environmental Trust. 'I was no longer able to tolerate the Duchy of Cornwall's completely insensitive attitude,' he wrote, adding that the Trust had lost all credibility in the eyes of the islanders.

On the day it ran Frank's statement, the doughty local broadsheet *Scilly up to Date* mischievously trailed a quote from Prince Charles, Duke of Cornwall, directly above Frank's photograph:

> We must forever remain vigilant against the threatening forces
> of change. . . For various reasons we have allowed terrible damage
> to be inflicted on parts of this country's unique landscape.
> H.R.H. Prince Charles

Ask Frank his profession, and he might quite likely tell you 'shopkeeper'. And certainly there is a part of Frank that is proud to be a humble island trader, bedded in the community, selling his wedding pictures and his postcards and books of local photographs across the counter and hearing the till ring, as it has rung for the three previous generations of Gibson forebears, on Scilly and in Penzance.

'Nothing gives me greater pleasure than seeing a picture I've taken leave the wall of my shop knowing it will end up on someone else's,' he assures me blandly. Conscious of his almost palpable intensity, I doubt whether this is the sum of his ambition. But then a lot of artists protect themselves that way, I reflect: conceal their creativity behind a mask of genial commerciality.

His success – he assures me in the same healthy top-of-the-morning tone – derives from knowing exactly what his customers want, then going out of his way to provide it.

How exactly? I ask.

And gradually a rather different Frank appears.

By knowing where the tide is at any moment of the day or night, he replies – though of course, he adds, tides are in any Scillonian's blood, they have to be. By knowing where the light is, and where to be when, if you want to catch that vital one-time shot of a flower at its peak in a three-year cycle. Or knowing the one day of the year when a low autumn sun will strike a certain patch of sand, giving it that extra touch of gold that makes the difference.

A photograph must have a *story*, he continues with a rush of conviction. It must have *lift*. *Lift* in Frank's book is a lightness of texture, a separation of shadows. Bad printing can kill lift. So can a wrong exposure, he explains.

Then, as suddenly as he has appeared, Frank the dedicated photographer disappears again, and we are back with Frank the shopkeeper. To stay abreast of his customers, he says, he keeps a close eye on which of his postcards sell, and which stick in the rack. In France, he has noted on his visits there, the customers are prepared to go for arty. Frank has seen postcards in Brittany with nothing but an anchor and a bit of sea and sky in the background, and they're selling like hot cakes.

But English tourists, Frank goes on in the strange, teasing voice he has, they're more conservative, you see, and arty isn't what they're about to buy *at all*. Your English tourist likes a picture to have everything in it, doesn't he? He likes the whole plate filled, Frank explains, referring to the large-format camera he prefers for landscape. Frank would quite like to do arty himself, he admits. But your English tourist won't be bothered with arty. So that's pretty well that.

And he gives me a nice smile.

And if I had allowed the conversation to rest there – well, I just might have come away thinking: Frank Gibson is what he says he is, a journeyman photographer, a shopkeeper, an efficient taker of wedding pictures and colour postcards for your English tourist who won't be bothered with arty.

But I'd have been dead wrong. Because Frank Gibson is a series of very well-protected Chinese boxes, and up till now he has only allowed me to open a couple of them. Like his pictures, Frank needs time and patience, or there's no story and no lift.

We are standing in the Aladdin's cave where the Gibson treasure is stored, and Frank is its keeper. It is half shed, half amateur laboratory, a litter of cluttered shelves, ancient equipment, boxes, printer's blocks and books. Many hundreds of plates and thousands of old photographs are still awaiting an inventory. Most have never seen the light of day. Any agent, publisher or accountant would go into free fall at the very sight of them. Is there not a booming market in old photographs, as Frank must surely know? Of course there is! Why else would Gibson photographs, whether in copyright or out, be dismally colported across the globe without payment or acknowledgement?

But Frank has heard all this before. Occasionally, he confesses, he has pondered legal action. But not, it seems, for very long.

Why not?

He pulls an uncomfortable smile. Well, some newspapers and publishers play straight, no question, he insists. As to the villains, well, yes, he agrees — speaking somehow against his own inclination — something should be done. After all, the pictures are worth a bit, aren't they? And there are the children to think of, naturally. . .

But his otherwise combative nature is not in the fight, and the reason, so far as I can fathom, lies somewhere deep inside his island soul. When you live on the islands, you do things the island way, not London's. If you want to spend your life scrambling after money, do it somewhere else. And really that's about it, thank you, his expression says, as he puts the locks back on the shed door.

Who taught you composition? I ask him as we walk. Walking is much better than sitting. Frank gets stiff sitting. Best to keep on the move. We're passing St. Mary's Hospital. It has fourteen beds and Frank reckons it's the best hospital in the world, for as long as those bureaucrats on the mainland don't ruin it. And Frank should know. Four years ago, crippled with rheumatism, he saw the inside of several hospitals and, as I have learned elsewhere, fought his way back with a stoical bravery that his friends still talk about with awe.

Your father? I ask. Your grandfather? Who taught you?

Frank is fiercely indignant at the notion that his father taught him his skills. *No one*, he replies vigorously. My father and I never talked about *anything* like that. It's instinct. And experience, naturally. You get to know what a good picture is, foreground, middle ground, background. Instinct, plus a bit of looking at other photographers' work, which is only natural.

Which other photographers? I ask.

Whereupon a list comes out of him as readily as if he were naming his favourite footballers — except that not all the photographers that Frank names enjoy his uncritical admiration.

So it transpires that the same Frank Gibson who likes nothing better than to supply his customers with what they want possesses a collection of photographic books and is, among other things, a devoted fan of Don McCullin's war pictures.

So what's Don doing now? he asks me excitedly, when I tell him I have met McCullin a few times. When I last heard of him, I say, he was photographing the Mendip Hills.

Frank's eyes light up. Black-and-white? he asks.

I believe so, I reply.

Good man, he says.

'Colour photography, it's not *real* photography at all,' Frank declares as we stride along. 'Real photography is about light, not colour. And what I'm going to do with my so-called retirement, I'm getting back to basics: black-and-white.'

And he won't be handing over his pictures to be developed and printed by a computerised machine any more, he adds disdainfully. He'll do it all himself, in his own dark-room, all the stages. In order to be sure of the quality, he says. To be in control of his own life again.

The Scillies are his element, he explains simply. Later he puts the same thought in a letter to me: 'I should have elaborated a bit more on this subject. Ansel Adams has his Yosemite Valley. Fay Godwin does her best work in the hills of Great Britain. I have my islands with their unique granite outcrops which can be awesome in different lights, and the ever-changing seascapes which can be quite dramatic in winter.'

We have come a long way from the man who talks of anchors on a blue field.

'I'd like to be the same as John,' he announces gravely, speaking of his great-grandfather and the first of the photographic Gibsons. Then he uses John's phrase as if it were his own: '*Portraying events which later become history.*'

And somewhere around here he lets drop the word *re-enactment*.

I do a double take. *Re-enactment*? I repeat. Surely he can't be saying that like his forebears he will *re-enact* events, pose his subjects in their doorways, on a tin mine, a hillside or a sea shore? That hardly fits in with the modern concept of photo-journalism, I suggest, recalling his recent admiration of McCullin.

'It wouldn't bother me one bit,' Frank retorts. 'I wouldn't mind that *at all*.'

He'd do it just the way great-grandfather John did it a hundred-and-something years ago, he repeats: re-enactment and portraying future history.

We are on the outskirts of Hugh Town. The wrong outskirts. Down by the harbour, Hugh Town has one of the prettiest high streets you could wish to see: mostly Victorian, some Regency, granite, all beautifully to scale. But what has happened since recalls the worst of South-East English subtopia – except that the poverty of design and the high cost of bringing materials to the island ensure an even lower standard.

And suddenly either my presence, or something I have said, triggers Frank's fury and he is launched on a veritable tirade against the mindlessness of what is happening to St. Mary's in particular, and to the islands in general: the needless proliferation of motorcars – almost one for every two residents, and double yellow lines to match – the perpetual feuding between the islanders that makes a mockery of local autonomy – the carpetbaggers and developers from the mainland with their ideas for making a quick buck – these and more receive the rough side of Frank's tongue, until his passion cools and we talk about other things.

All the same, I am left reflecting that, like every Gibson before him, Frank has committed his life to photographing a world that is slipping away from him even while he watches it – this drowning Scilly landscape, this vanishing culture that was vanishing when great-grandfather John first brought his camera here, and today is sunk so deep that it must sometimes seem to Frank and his fellow islanders that only the tip of the mast is showing above the waterline. And surely the burden of recording angel must lie heavier on Frank than on any of his predecessors, for the reason that the cultural and social decline that each Gibson successively observed has in Frank's lifetime reached its nadir and fulfilment.

The industries that once gave the islands their slender livelihood are no longer dying but dead. And it's poor old Frank who has to represent the family at the funeral. The only survivor is the murderous octopus of tourism, as another precious part of our heritage is gathered inexorably into theme-park England.

'My dad lived with a chip on his shoulder,' Frank declares suddenly, as if he were excusing him for something. 'Maybe his early childhood was to blame. He wasn't demonstrative. Not at all. My mother was a far more gentle soul. I hope to God that's what's rubbed off on me. She was a bloody saint, I reckon, to live with him for all those years. Island-born, of course. No one ever asks about my mother's father. He was a stone mason. You go round the local churches, you'll see all these gravestones signed J. F. Ellis. That's my grandfather.'

We visit the old churchyard. It is mastered at one point by a fine war memorial to the fallen of the 1914-18 war. On the plinth we find the graven signature of J. F. Ellis.

'I loved that man,' says Frank. 'If I'd ever had a boy I'd have called him John Francis. Well, we didn't, but we had a daughter and I called her Janette Frances, which was as near as we could get.'

I ask him how he is as a grandfather. It seems easier than asking how he was as a father. He laughs – but at himself, not at me. 'I yell at them,' he confesses. 'If they're good, I'm all right. But if they're bad, I yell.'

And I can't help feeling, that's what his father did to Frank. Or maybe his father just wanted to, and didn't. And that fathers are very big figures in the Gibson line. Powerful men, inward, disciplinarian and withheld, visionaries determined to be workmen, imbued with the Methodist puritanism that, among believers and unbelievers alike, is the heritage of the Cornish Wesleyan revival.

'Launceston was an absolute waste of time,' says Frank. He is speaking of Launceston College where he went as a boarder after his brother won a scholarship there. I too remember Launceston. We used to play rugger against them when I was at Sherborne, and they were even more barbaric than we were. 'They taught me absolutely nothing. My education stopped dead after I learned the three Rs. We were lucky with our children. They could stay here till they were sixteen and learn our standards. After that it was up to them.'

Another victim of the English boarding school system, I thought: join the club.

'Events that will one day become history,' says Frank, echoing great-grandfather John.

The Scillies these days are sold to tourists as Britain's fortunate islands, and so they are if you are looking for a couple of weeks of hypnotic natural beauty, seclusion, superb beaches, early flowers, cold seas, island walks, seals, flowers, birds migrant and resident, about a thousand archaeological sites and some of the most beautiful coastline on earth.

There is no sweeter air on earth than Scilly air. The silence out of season is absolute, whether you come from London or Penzance. One man's footsteps passing through Hugh Town on a still November night sound like the coming of a vengeance. Thanks to the Gulf Stream, the temperature variation over an entire year is seldom more than around 10 degrees Centigrade.

Nevertheless you do not have to look about you for long, or read much local history, before the islands also impart a sense of unstoppable human tragedy. Misfortune, not fortune, marks their story.

By the 1870s when John Gibson began portraying his 'events that will become history', the industrial revolution was already sounding the death-knell for Scilly's tenuous economy. There were fine shipyards on St. Mary's: but only for building and repairing wooden ships. The kelp industry, once a mainstay of glass manufacture and the chemical industries, was history already. Science had replaced it. Small farming kept the islanders self-sufficient but brought next-to-nothing in the way of cash. The unlikely exception was the flower industry, begun in 1870, four years after the railway line from London to Penzance was opened for goods. By a miracle of ingenious management and collective hard work, Scilly's early flowers have prevailed against fierce competition to this day.

The Scilly fishing industry also survived – but only on borrowed time, and always in competition with the mainland fleets from Newlyn and St. Ives. Scillonian fishermen, they say, were too pious to fish on Sundays, which was how those heathens from St. Ives stole a march on them. St. Ives fishermen are quite as pious as they should be, of course, but Scillonians tend to see all mainlanders, even the Cornish, as predators.

The Cornish mainland where John Gibson had his shop was faring little better. The Cornish mining industry had been killed off by cheap tin from the colonies. The once-great trading ports of Hayle and Falmouth, like those of Scilly, were no longer needed. Hayle silted up. *Man*, writes Barbara Tuchman in 'The Proud Tower', *had entered the nineteenth century using his own and animal power. . . He entered the twentieth with his capacities in transportation, communication, production, manufacture and weaponry multiplied a thousandfold by the energy of machines.*

By the turn of the century, the energy of these machines had wrecked the local shipping industry and driven thousands of Cornish labourers from the land. Yet Cornwall had no alternative employment to offer, any more than it has now. The exodus of the young continues unabated, whether from West Cornwall or from Scilly. Some in middle age return, having made their fortunes – or not.

Today Cornwall's *per capita* income ticks over at 70 per cent of the national average. Though government figures put the number lower, real unemployment runs as high as 40 per cent in some regions, and seldom sinks below 17 per cent. Out-of-town supermarkets, low earnings and excessive business taxes have produced a string of ghost towns. The 1996 'Penzance Town Centre Study' tells us that there are forty-five 'vacant units' at the present time in Penzance. For 'vacant unit' read empty shop.

Ten years ago during the mackerel boom, Cornish and Scillonian inshore fishermen were obliged to watch foreign factory ships hoovering more fish from their traditional fishing grounds than they themselves were permitted to take in a year. Subsequent international and European Union legislation has been too little, too partisan, too late and too lame to halt the ruin, and the Cornish fishermen feel bitterly betrayed by Westminster. Fish and seafood stocks are diminishing at a disastrous rate.

The boom industry on the mainland is crime – committed, we are told, mostly by young people with a drug habit to feed. Some have never seen their fathers work. It will take more than a Cornish university to give them back their chances.

Today John Gibson's worst fears are realised. Perhaps it is no coincidence that the shipwreck has become the symbol of the Gibson family's work.

Frank and I decide on a modest re-enactment of the difficulties the early Gibsons faced when in 1874 Alexander, Frank's grandfather, clambered onto Peninnis Head, St. Mary's, to photograph the wreck of the 845-ton *Minnehaha* (plate 22), a three-masted wooden ship out of Falmouth bound for Dublin, laden with *guano* from Peru. She had foundered in fog on her way to the approaches of St. Mary's Roads with the loss of half her crew.

Peninnis Head lies at the eastern side of the main channel into Hugh Town, and about half an hour's walk from the town centre. Frank has put a brass and mahogany half-plate camera in his rucksack, a Thornton Pickard Ruby. Alexander used such a camera for the shot. Maybe this very one. Frank possesses no mahogany tripod, so we make do with a modern tubular alloy job.

How the Gibsons would have got word of the wreck is anybody's guess, but their determination to be first at the scene presupposes an efficient intelligence network both in Scilly and on the Cornish mainland. On St. Mary's, clearly, there was no great problem: the islanders, like the coastal villagers of West Penwith, have an uncanny instinct for a wreck, and word seems to travel without human aid.

But on the mainland they would have had to work harder for their information, and the dash to the scene would have been dramatic and elaborate – not least because there was no enlarging process in those days, which meant that a print could only be as big as the plate from which it was taken.

Vying with each other for the biggest picture – and therefore the greatest prominence at art exhibitions – photographers provided themselves with cameras so enormous they had to be horse-drawn. To this impedimenta must be added a box full of heavy brass-tubed lenses, an apothecary's den of bottles and pans, and the nightmare of wet-plate developing on site in portable dark-rooms improvised from carts or tents.

Our Thornton Pickard Ruby measures no more than a modest foot square when closed. Nevertheless Alexander Gibson would have been accompanied by a handful of assistants, including no doubt his younger brother Herbert, 13. Alexander was by now 17. Both boys were born to photography – Alexander was taking pictures at such an early age that he had to be set on a stool to focus. Both, like Frank, never thought to follow any other profession. Both – like all the Gibsons, one suspects – did what their father told them. Most likely, their helpers would have been kids like themselves, fired by the excitement of the chase.

Yet however quick Alexander was, and however well attended, by the time he reached the headland he could be sure of finding the usual crowd of spectators who gather like seagulls out of nowhere as soon as they scent a wreck. Some even made it into the picture.

Frank and I decided to assume that, because the wreck had happened so close to the Gibsons' house, Alexander had made up his photographic plates in advance. If so, the pressure upon him and his team was all the greater, since the plates, once coated with wet collodion, had only about an hour's life – though John Gibson on a different occasion was known to have bought himself extra time by wrapping his plates in towels dipped in sea water.

Our walk ends with a scramble over descending boulders to a sloping granite platform beneath a promontory called Jolly Rock on the outer head of Peninnis. The surface of the granite is wet and slippery and about twelve feet wide, with a sheer fall to the sea. It is split by a cleft two feet wide that descends to boiling surf. Frank steps broad, like a seaman on a rolling deck, while I follow with the tripod. As a child he played here barefoot, he assures me cheerfully. Well *I* didn't. And I don't like heights, least of all when I have no tread to my shoes. But heights don't bother Frank – though he does remember having a bad turn coming down from the top of Bishop Light. As well he might, seeing that the Bishop Lighthouse, even before you count the new helipad, stands 167 feet from base to vane (plate 87), and is the tallest lighthouse in the British Isles.

South winds produce a blinding sea-spray at Peninnis Head. The force of the sea has bored under the

FRANK GIBSON, 1996. PHOTOGRAPH BY JOHN le CARRÉ

rock and ripped away protrusions, leaving only stumps. If the *Minnehaha* went down in fog, then the odds are, no storm was blowing. And mercifully, no storm is blowing today: just a light drizzle on a dull November afternoon, and the restless seething of the sea below. Yet as Frank mounts the camera on the tripod and selects a lens, the camera seems to draw both wind and rain.

A little breathless, eyes alight, Frank explains the ground rules above the clatter of the sea: the whole plate must be used and the picture composed at the time of taking. No cropping will be possible in the dark-room, no selecting one part of the negative. The choice of lens – varying only in focal length – is crucial. Exposure is a matter of a few seconds, counted by instinct and experience.

Frank bounds to the front of the camera, removes the lens cap, bounds to the back and spirits a black cloth over his head while I watch the camera rocking in the negligible breeze, and wonder aloud how on earth grandfather Alexander would have managed all this in a force eight gale. Answer: with one lot of helpers hanging on to him, and another lot holding down the camera. And it crosses my mind as I continue watching Frank that men who live around the sea make natural photographers: in their handling of tackle, in their watchfulness and patience, in their intense and secretive observation of the world around them, and their respectful awareness of the laws of nature.

The black cloth, with its faded crimson lining for the benefit of wedding guests, lends Frank a conjuror's magic. Perched on the cliff before me, with the darkening sea for background, he resembles one of the early Gibsons' heroically posed extras, a hooded Byron braving nature's wrath. Still hidden from my view, he reports his actions. He is studying the focusing screen. He is composing his picture upside-down, which is how the screen delivers it. His arm flies up: the shot is composed. Throwing aside the cloth, he strides to the front of the camera, replaces the lens cap, returns to the back and inserts a mahogany frame containing the prepared glass plate. He whisks the wooden screen from the frame and, having thus exposed the plate, darts to the front of the camera yet again and whips off the lens cap.

A thousand-and-one, a thousand-and-two, a thousand-and-three . . . I try to imagine Alexander's helpers holding their breath and praying as they struggle to wrestle the camera still for these vital seconds. Reckoning the exposure complete, Frank replaces the lens cap. We relax and take each other's photographs with a more modern camera while there is still light.

But Alexander and his team would have enjoyed no such respite. For them, it was all haste once more as they tore back to the laboratory. The collodion is drying on the glass! Sensitivity is diminishing! Once inside the lab, however, Alexander can use the slowness of the process to his advantage. The plate can be developed 'by inspection'. If an image threatens to form too fast, the plate can be dunked in cold water to slow it down.

And once the plate is dry, there is another transformation that takes place in the laboratory, though it is a less happy one. Weak shadows can be strengthened with intensifier. Overbright patches can be toned down with ferri-cyanide. Cloud formations and passing birds can enliven an empty sky. By these and similar methods, Alexander Gibson the photographer is about to become Alexander Gibson the great landscape painter, claiming his place in that most questionable of artistic pantheons: English romantic painting of the nineteenth century.

Though Thomas Hardy might write of English rural life grappling with the turbulence of change, Charles Dickens might portray thieves and harlots, public executions, the abuse of children, the plight of the poor and the corruption of justice – though the Industrial Revolution might be tearing into British society, raising hopes, dashing or fulfilling them, enriching and enslaving, wrecking settled lives and communities, devastating countryside, swelling cities and causing social displacement on a scale not seen since the Civil Wars of two hundred years before – though poverty and famine abound, workhouses are crowded out and factory conditions appalling – the mainstream of our national English painting in Victorian times is stuck with an idealised, escapist, cosmetic view of life that best expresses itself in a noble stag posing on a Scottish moor.

If there were distinguished exceptions who refused to bow to this tyranny of post-Napoleonic retrenchment, it was still left to a brave few, and to 'common caricaturists' such as Cruikshank, to render society's realities with anything approaching the force of their literary contemporaries.

And the Newlyn Society of Artists, to which the Gibsons and other local photographers now gravitated, was not in the business of dissent. Like all painters, its members wanted their pictures to be displayed, appreciated and bought. They did not stand apart from the great Victorian dream of retrenchment, respectability and peace – why should they? They were creatures of their time. They were ambitious. They had a living to make. They were artists. They were enjoying themselves. If the reigning warlords of the London art establishment were bent upon banishing anything that might offend the proprieties, then so be it: the Newlyn artists would play the game. Today, of course, the prevailing bigotry works the other way, and our art bureaucrats strive to banish anything that gives comfort to conventional sensitivities. The Newlyn Gallery still provides an honourable showcase for local painters, many of whom work within traditional lines. Yet its most celebrated exhibit of recent years was the image of a urinating standing woman projected continuously onto a television screen. She was part of a travelling American exhibition, and she came to Newlyn courtesy of the Arts Council, from which Newlyn, alone of all Cornish art galleries, receives regular financial support. But if the gallery's managers thought they were doing anything innovative, they were deluding themselves. Newlyn in the nineties, exactly as in the nineteenth century, was taking its cue from the metropolitan art establishment. It was the same old dictatorship, got up in different clothes.

In the nineteenth century, few Cornish artists were indigenous. Most were affluent middle-class immigrants with an idealised view of local life. As painters, they were more concerned with light and colour than with society, and in Cornwall they found light and colour galore. For company they clung to one another, and for guidance they looked first to London, and only cautiously at other art capitals.

And London's message, though never articulated in as many words, was plain for all to see. You may paint a cow, but it must be a healthy cow, plump, ruminative and placid: in short, a middle-class cow. Naked girls should be provided with wings and a diaphanous night-dress and appointed Vestals of the Shades. Naked boys, interestingly, were deemed more respectable. But if you are moved to render common labourers, be sure to endow them with an acceptance of their condition and respect for their superiors. Common children may be painted barefoot provided they are portrayed as beaming scamps.

The greatest Empire nation in the world, in the throes of the world's greatest industrial revolution, was not minded to air its own shortcomings. The radicalism and cultural adventurism that had followed in Napoleon's wake across continental Europe and into Russia must never taint these sceptred shores.

And that went for art too. Quite particularly for art. In a world struggling with illiteracy as well as radicalism, the seditious power of imagery was not ignored.

How much of this rubbed off on the new breed of 'photographic artist' is plain enough to see from this book. John Gibson seems to have confined his painting to elaborate retouching of his photographs. But where John tidged, the fiery Alexander saw himself as a fully-fledged landscape artist and, when he couldn't get the photograph, painted a picture instead. The results were efficient, imitative and uninspired.

But the real miracle is that, by and large, John Gibson and his successors, having cheerfully accepted the straitjacket of contemporary painting, prevailed so splendidly against it. Photographs were posed, yes; attitudes were struck, misery was ignored in favour of a brave smile. Too often, photographers aspired to create a painterly masterpiece rather than report what they saw, and the Gibsons were not immune to this temptation. The interaction between painters and their photographic imitators was at times so close that you are tempted to ask who was looking over whose shoulder: the painter over the photographer's or the other way round?

There is a story I have not yet been able to track down that Alexander Gibson was actually under contract to the painters of the Newlyn School. To do what, in that case? Provide them with 'aids' from which to paint? Or to photograph their paintings for them, which in those days was the only known form of reproduction? It hardly matters. The new photographers homed naturally on whatever was around them: etchings, paintings, theatre – and the prevailing middle-class passion for '*tableaux vivants*', or in other words: '*re-enactment*'.

What matters is that the Gibsons, however much they tried to conform with these early reactionary influences, brought an historical truth, and an awareness of life and death to their work, that often exceeded the reach of the painters they aspired to join. In the end, perhaps, as so often in England, it was a matter of class. The majority of Newlyn painters were of the middle to upper class. The photographers in the main were artisans. Manual labour was not alien to them. Where the painters watched and imagined, the photographers knew what they were portraying, because they had lived it.

The Gibsons lived life where the Newlyn Society formed its own cricket team, acted plays to itself and observed its adopted world with the eyes of art. But the Gibsons' first loyalty was to the community that bore them, as it is Frank's today. If an islander tomorrow were for some reason to become a target of prurient media interest, as has happened once or twice in the past, Fleet Street would get no help from Frank, no matter how big the cheque they offered. He lives here. He's one of them. He shares their secrets, lives their life. He has children of his own.

And his forebears would have responded no differently, you can be sure. The Gibson continuum is more than just a camera passing from father to son for four generations. It is a loyalty and above all a duty to West Cornwall and the islands.

Leafing through these photographs, you cease to ask yourself which member of the family took this shot or that one – whether it was John or Alexander or James or even Frank. The family quarrels were not about who did what, or about casting out the old and bringing in the new. No turbulent rising star of a new generation seized his camera, slung his toggle-bag over his shoulder and marched into the sunset vowing to become a Cartier-Bresson, a Don McCullin or a Snowdon. The Gibsons, in Barbara Tuchman's phrase, may have graduated from animal power to the moonshot, from the wet-plate camera to the all-electronic single-lens reflex. Yet they have pursued the same trade in the same place in the same way without ever once mistaking technique for substance.

Scillonians know things they are barely aware of knowing. That cormorants fish alone, and shags in groups. That grey seals puff up their necks to give themselves a lifebelt while they doze. That peregrine falcons feast on passing racing pigeons, leaving only their heads and ringed legs lying on the rocks. Scillonians are heir to Bronze Age villages, burial chambers, shrines, menhirs, the spirits of drowned sailors, Roman settlements. In their native memory are off-islands populated by seamen's widows, streets once occupied entirely by smugglers and a row of houses built from the profits of a single German wreck.

In Scilly, say the wits, the clocks go backwards. But Frank Gibson knows that the opposite is true. And as an islander and an inheritor, he is pledged to record events that will become history all too soon.

The Mount's Bay Studio in Penzance

A CENTURY OF IMAGES
REX COWAN

'Two shall be grinding at the mill, the one shall be taken and the other left.'

It is said that when Herbert Gibson was buried in St. Mary's on the Isles of Scilly in June 1937 his brother and partner in their photographic business, Alexander, was so distraught that he nearly threw himself into the grave. It was the end of a passionate familial and professional relationship that had assembled some of the most vivid images that the new craft of photography practised by the brothers could produce. The text of Alexander's graveside eulogy illuminates the sketchy information available about the life and work of these two men, the most prodigious of an unusually productive dynasty of photographers which is now in its fifth generation.

Alexander describes the aims of their craft, producing from as 'long ago as the sixties of the last century . . . a series of photographs *so that strangers might see* (my italics) what wonders this little known archipelago held in a concentrated form of artistic and scientific interest: archaeology, geology, nature studies, flower culture in all its detail, wild bird and seal life, village homes and customs, ancient Megalithic remains and local trades of ship-building, spinning and weaving, thatching and straw making.' Add to that the drama, pathos and striking forms of shipwrecks, and of everyday events, and you could be describing the activity and purpose of each one of this remarkable family of photographers – right up to today.

Trying to unravel the complex relationships of the Gibson family is not easy. Family rivalries have resulted in much information being lost, forgotten or withheld. It is ironic that the Gibsons, who were all busy recording other people's lives and work, should have revealed so little about themselves. The moves between Scilly and Penzance, and the changes in proprietorship of the business, are inevitably confusing for anyone trying to trace their fortunes. Their eccentricities have been interpreted as evidence of either talent or awkwardness by friends and observers. Within the limitations of a short introductory text to the lives of four generations of talented individualists over a period of one hundred years, accuracy is not easy. I have tried to get dates and places right, and I hope that any errors will not detract from the main thrust of my story of this unique family.

Gibson photography originated with John Gibson. Born in 1827 on one of the Aran Islands, he came from a family whose roots in St. Martins, one of the Isles of Scilly, go back to the seventeenth century. His father, James Gibson, had joined the coastguard service and was posted to Inishmore, one of the Irish Aran Islands where John had a truncated childhood, going to sea at the age of twelve. His father died a year later, in 1840, and was buried in Ireland; but his death is remembered in a graveyard in Penzance where John's mother Catherine is buried, and where John himself is described as 'Pioneer Photographer in Penzance and the Isles of Scilly'.

Only sketchy anecdotes survive to explain John's eventual involvement in photography. The most exotic tale is that he purchased a camera abroad, maybe in China, on one of his many voyages and was enchanted by the new technology of preserving images, despite the cumbersome nature of the equipment and the laborious efforts required to expose and develop the photographs. Like all the Gibsons to follow, he was remembered for his forceful personality, and would have been well suited to take his father's place and look after both business and his widowed mother. Shortly after James's death, the family – John, his mother Catherine, and three sisters, travelling from

SAILING SHIPS OFF ST. MARY'S (GIBSON, *c.* 1880).

ST MARY'S, *c.* 1880. BOATS FILL THE HARBOUR.

Ireland by boat and pony and trap – returned to Scilly. Here they opened a general store which sold a range of items from fancy goods to meat, but John, restless as ever, went back to sea, for adventure and to supplement his income. Somewhere, after buying his camera, he learnt the elements of photography. There were establishments in Falmouth, Truro and, later, Penzance that held classes in 'art', teaching photography in the late 1850s; and as Charles Thomas* has recalled, in that era photography occupied a position in education that straddled art and science.

The early practitioners saw photography as a development of an existing art form. Fox Talbot, in his address to the Royal Society on 31 January 1839 ('Some Account of the Art of Photogenic Drawing', although he used the term 'photography' in his patent), described it as the 'Process by which Natural objects may be made to delineate themselves without the aid of the Artist's Pencil'. In the directories of the period (Kelly's and the Post Office), the term 'Photographic artist' was used for most of the photographers listed.

Two other pioneers of photography lived and worked in Penzance at the time, William Brooks and Robert Preston. Charles Thomas links them with John Gibson, and confirms that they worked together, using Preston's facilities at No. 1 South Terrace, Penzance, not far from the Promenade where John later opened his first Penzance branch (see frontispiece). It is quite possible that John served some sort of apprenticeship or teaching arrangement with the younger but equally dedicated Robert Preston. This would account for the speed with which he learnt the photographic business when he was nearing middle age. These photographers collaborated, and probably went on photographic expeditions together, but they also became keen competitors.

The Isles of Scilly are an archipelago of approximately 200 islands and large rocks lying twenty-five miles west by south of Land's End, Cornwall. Only five of them are now inhabited, but several others were populated during the seventeenth and eighteenth centuries. Lying athwart the trade routes at the apex of the English and St. George's Channels, they were a vital shelter and lay-by for ships homeward bound from the Atlantic or the Indies, or encountering contrary winds. Sometimes there were as many as 300 ships of every size and nationality crowding the roadsteads during bad weather. At the time of John's return to Scilly, the islands were experiencing a period of relative prosperity under the autocratic reign of Augustus Smith, the Lord Proprietor of the Islands, who held

* Charles Thomas: *Views and Likenesses. Photographers and Their Work in Cornwall and Scilly, 1839-1870.* Truro, 1988.

them under lease from the Duchy of Cornwall for a term of ninety-nine years from 1834 at an annual rental of £40. Scilly had in 1852 already been through a period of economic distress, with poverty in the off-islands, and Augustus Smith, or 'The Governor' as he was called locally, had started to transform the islands, economically, socially and educationally. At his own expense he set up free schools for all children on the islands, halted smuggling, introduced new breeds of cattle and sheep, and cultivated the famous tropical gardens on the island of Tresco. There he built the Abbey, a house of his own design whose large state rooms faced south, with a magnificent view. To complete his idea of paradise, he bred ostriches to wander the grounds.

It is not clear why John didn't stay put in Scilly and mind the shop with his mother, instead of returning to sea. It was, after all, an expanding economy, with increasing agriculture and a developing annual tourist pilgrimage to the islands. His marriage to Sarah Gendall of St. Mary's in 1855 further cemented his links with Scilly. In the parish record of the marriage he is described as 'seaman of St. Mary's'. Sarah too came from a seagoing family, and her lineage includes one poignant irony. In 1736 Alexander Gendal (*sic*) was shipwrecked and drowned on a journey in a small boat from Penzance to Scilly: Sarah's two sons were to become the foremost photographers of shipwreck disasters in the world. Another ancestor, Captain Alexander Gendall of St. Mary's, was the master of the *Prudence and Jane*, a sloop which in 1793, also on a voyage from Penzance to Scilly, was driven by contrary winds to Cherbourg. After his marriage John went to Penzance, an urge he was often unable to resist during his lifetime, settling there during the early 1860s.

There has always been a migration from Scilly to Penzance and West Penwith, a district of southwest Cornwall. Penzance was a thriving market town, and it attracted (as it does today) those with ambitions which could not be realised in the parochial environment of the islands. Cornwall was noted for the unusual number of commercial photographers practising west of Falmouth from the earliest beginnings of photography in the 1850s. Clusters of photographers were sited on the coast from Truro to Penzance. Many probably came because of the proximity of the Royal Cornwall Polytechnic Society of Falmouth, which held lectures and exhibitions, and promoted the new 'art' of photography and the technical developments of the times. The coming of the Great Western Railway in 1852, bringing with it business and the growth of an early tourist industry, may also have attracted professional photographers, although Cornwall was far from having great wealth. Indeed some of its industries were already in decline. By the 1860s thousands of tin and copper miners were out of work and mines closed down every month. Production of copper and tin fell dramatically, and the air was no longer full of the sound of the pumping house engines. Villages and mine installations emptied, and within a decade the industry collapsed, to become artefacts of industrial archaeology, gaunt, cathedral-like remains to be recorded in haunting images by the Gibson cameras.

What rewarding places Scilly and Cornwall were for the photographer! Both were wreathed in history and legend, romanticism and the harsh reality of the industrial age: Cornwall with its rugged landscapes, hidden coves, and fishing villages clinging to the hilly coasts; Scilly with the Atlantic battering its host of small islands, 'slight rafts or platforms surrounded by an immensity of sea, and arched by an even greater immensity of sky'. And everywhere the always changing light and colour, the changing shapes and contours of the landscape.

The coasts and shoal areas of both places were also minefields for the scores of ships that were cast up and wrecked on rock and shore, each year. Great schooners and small fishing boats, liners and Indiamen, people, animals and cargo all succumbed to the brutality of nature – the sea and rocks were no respecters of size or strength or importance. Each wreck was a drama, and a battle, with its heroes and cowards, its winners and losers. And for them all the Gibsons were there, during or after the event, with their cameras.

John Gibson established himself with a studio in the Promenade at Penzance shortly after he went there around 1860. He took portraits and built up an archive of pictures of local views, people and events. The building was demolished in 1883. John carried on business as 'Gibson Photographer' in this shop on the seafront underneath the Royal Baths Boarding & Lodging House. The title of the business was to be a subject of bitter dispute within the family in later years. Outside the shop/studio can be seen four boards with prints drying in the sun, and eleven photographs are displayed in the window. This print (see frontispiece) must have been made some years after 1879 as it is signed on the back 'Gibson & Sons'. Around 1865, John returned to Scilly. He had never been able to resist the feeling of belonging to the Islands. He did, however, keep a toehold in Penzance, though it is not clear whether he then retained the shop in the Promenade. Scilly had no resident photographer, so he had the monopoly, whereas in Penzance there was keen competition from other photographers. It has been difficult to identify the early photographs taken by John in the 1860s in Scilly. Some are dated by the events. Plate 77, from the general appearance of Augustus Smith compared with an earlier photograph by another photographer, William Jenkyns, was made around 1865. Plate 4, from the state of the boat-building on Porthcressa Beach, is probably from 1869. After 1870 the dates are confirmable.

John's two sons were Alexander Gendall Gibson, born in Scilly in 1857, and Herbert Gibson, born in 1861. They were to build on their father's achievement as a pioneer in photography and form a partnership which produced work of the extraordinary range and quality reflected in this book. Both were taught the art of photography by their father – taught at first to see it as a novelty and as a magical craft. From the shop and post office their parents ran in Silver Street, they watched and later learnt how to take, process and sell photographs. Alexander (and probably Herbert) went to the infant school in Church Street (Plate 60), and then to Carn Thomas School, where from that dreamy setting on a hill overlooking a turquoise bay they could watch the boats and fishermen that were to form the subject matter of many of their photographs.

The death of John's wife Sarah at the age of 38 in 1871 could have destabilised the Gibson family. Within the space of two years John had lost the two most important women in his life: his mother Catherine had died in 1869. Alexander, just 13, Herbert, 10, and three young sisters were now left in charge of their itinerant father. Into that vacuum stepped Miss Gendall, as the islanders called Sarah's spinster sister, who took over the children's upbringing. By this time Alexander was helping his father, carrying the heavy camera and developing equipment, focusing the lens, sometimes standing on a chair whilst his father arranged the composition of the scene, or following him on perilous expeditions over cliffs and pathways to catch the moments of disaster and death when ships met their end.

Alexander left school at 12, and immediately started to work full-time for his father. He was a true apprentice, quick to learn, and Herbert was close behind him. The early years were apparently happy ones, free of the conflict and feuding that were to bedevil the family in later generations. It was as if they were fused together, learning, experimenting, creating. The brothers were of different temperament: Alexander, mercurial, eccentric, somewhat of an exhibitionist; Herbert 'a worker', staider and duller. Whilst there are still people in Scilly who can remember Alexander, few recall Herbert. But Alexander's eulogy delivered at Herbert's graveside in 1937 speaks eloquently of the strength of their feelings for each other.

> I feel that I need no excuse for making familiar to you all this real life story of the wonderful bond
> of love that existed between us, so strong, so everlasting, that though he has passed out of earthly
> sight, 'Though he is gone for ever, And will not come again Homeward to any shore on any tide',
> not even death has broken it, we are still one in spirit . . . He had not one mean thought or instinct
> in his whole nature; he had all the gifts which go to make the stature of the perfect man.

So, when struggling to attribute the authorship of many of the photographs taken during their partnership, to allocate the degrees of skill and innovation, of creativity, even of guile, these words of Alexander's ring in my ears.

> Not even the bible story of David and Jonathan could equal in intensity our devotion to each
> other; from infancy right on to the end we were in unbroken and most intimate association, even
> to a telepathy of mind: the harmony between us was never marred by so much as one unpleasant
> word or look, never any rivalry, jealousy, or even uncertain thought to disturb the mirror-like
> surface of our partnership: a life-record and a long one indeed of two brothers living and working
> daily together in such perfect content which must be rare and can never be beaten.

ALEXANDER AND HERBERT GIBSON DID NOT MANAGE TO
PHOTOGRAPH THE DRAMATIC RESCUE BY ROCKET APPARATUS OF
THE CREW OF THE FRENCH BRIGANTINE *MINERVE*, DRIVEN ON TO
MORNING POINT, ST. MARY'S IN 1878; BUT ALEXANDER PAINTED
THE SCENE.

ALEXANDER GIBSON
PHOTOGRAPHED PIPER'S HOLE ON
TRESCO, THEN PAINTED IN DETAIL
LIKE THE BOAT FOR VISITORS TO ROW
ACROSS THE WATER IN THE CAVE.

THE GIBSON'S CART FOR DEVELOPING WET PLATES,
AT THE GURNARD'S HEAD MINE WORKS,
C. 1870 (DETAIL OF PLATE 119).

This is a remarkable account of a personal and professional unity that generated some of the most exceptional photographic images of the last and the present century. It is not possible here to do more than touch the surface of the true nature of their collaboration, in both the artistry and the technology of their work. Because they worked in harness and in harmony, it is difficult to attribute many of the photographs to either one of them. I suspect that they 'both ground at the mill', complementing and supplementing one another. It is no surprise to discover that they married sisters, the daughters of a farmer and fisherman, Henry Jenkins of 'Dial Rock', Tresco.

The equipment the Gibsons used followed the invention of the Collodion process in 1851, which superseded the early (but tricky to work) daguerreotype. With this method, the glass, chemically coated plate was exposed wet in the camera. The need to keep the plate wet until it was developed required an on-the-spot development system. Some photographers used a tent. We know the Gibsons employed a cart draped so that it was light-free. They have craftily left us to pick it out of one of their photographs of the disused mine works at Gurnard's Head (Plate 119). The field camera, which could take negatives up to 12in by 10in, with a firm tripod, several lenses and a quantity of plates, would not have weighed less than 50 lbs. As soon as the photograph was exposed, the plate, still wet, would be wrapped in a towel or special cloth and speedily (it had to be developed in the hour) taken to the developing cart or tent. After the invention in 1871 of gelatin emulsion using silver bromide, the wet plate fell into disuse and the Gibsons switched to the new dry plate method. Some of the photographs can be dated by identifying the method of development.

The sheer size and weight of the equipment made the task of photographing some events particularly difficult. The shipwreck photos, which all the Gibsons sought and for which they are universally renowned, must have been the most difficult. Scrambling up cliffs laden with equipment or climbing winding muddy pathways in inclement weather to the scene of a wreck would have been hazardous, and as many Scilly wrecks happened well offshore on remote rocks or islets, blustery boat trips to those places must have been worse. The exposure time required, from one to ten or more seconds depending on the intensity of light, forced the photographer to keep the camera steady; and the movement of the sea, people and boats necessitated the later retouching and embellishment with paint that characterises many of the Gibson photographs.

By the 1870s, John, Herbert and Alexander were working together. John or Alexander would compose the photograph, and the third member of the team – often Herbert – would operate the camera. The Gibson style of photographic composition is unmistakable. They understood how the juxtaposition of humans with inanimate objects could convey emotions, or direct attention to the importance of a scene, not just fill an empty space. When they wanted to people a scene they frequently used family members, greatly enhancing the drama of their landscape. For the photograph of the cave known as Piper's Hole on Tresco in Scilly they placed two men on the rocks at the entrance and two women (John's wife and her sister?) symmetrically on the boulders above, thus giving us an idea of size and scale that enhances the view. In this photograph, incidentally, we can also see what John looked like in his forties, and the young Alexander already wearing the velvet cap which was to become familiar. Herbert was left behind the camera to expose the plate, which is why I have tentatively attributed it to him. Or look at Plate 69. John Wesley, on his mission to Cornwall in 1762, was said to have packed 30,000 of the faithful, or the shortly to be converted, into Gwennap pit. Place just twelve people in that vast arena in four groups, with one curious onlooker behind the wall, and the emptiness is broken up, the eye does not tire of the space.

Their treatment of the victims of the *Mohegan* disaster illustrates the unflinching way in which the Gibsons approached death and tragedy. In Plate 34, the body of a woman victim lies in straw. Around the cart are a group of (male) onlookers; the camera has caught all of their conflicting feelings of fear, curiosity, and respect for a life lost. But the photographer has no such fear. For the rarely seen Plate 35 one of the Gibsons took the shrouds off the faces of the drowned, seeing the peace of that scene, that the sight of death need not be awful, and that those uncovered bodies *were* human. They must also have realised the furore that the picture would cause.

In its early days, professional photography was dominated by portraiture. There was little market for scenic reproduction, but wealthier people could afford to have their portraits made – as in the past only the wealthy could afford to have their portraits painted. Small wonder that photography was considered more as fine art than as mechanical science in those days. Indeed Alexander became a reasonably accomplished painter. He attended the School of Art which opened in 1880 in Morrab Road, and the Arcade at the top of Market Jew Street. If he missed a shipwreck he would paint it (Plate 16); if he couldn't get a good sky in a photograph, he would paint it in (Plate 11). The Gibson brothers well understood that their camera did not reproduce subjects as the human eye saw them. It acted much more like a painting, showing a panorama or great detail whereas the eye records a brief impression within its field of vision.

But as the photographs of death reveal, the Gibsons were also gifted photo-journalists and reporters. In 1869 a private corporation, the Scilly Isles Telegraph Company, laid a cable from Land's End to St. Mary's. It was not too soon. Hundreds of ships stopped at Scilly every year, dozens were wrecked on her shores. The only means of communication was by mail on a packet boat, and it could sometimes take a week for word to reach the mainland. When the telegraph arrived, the Gibsons saw it as a means of supplementing their photographic income. John became the local news correspondent; Alexander learnt Morse and was appointed as the island telegraphist. These two roles were combined during the catastrophic disaster of the wreck of the 3500-ton German passenger and mail steamer, *Schiller*, which in thick fog on 7 May 1875 struck the Retarrier Ledges off Scilly. Ironically, the islanders thought the ship's distress signals were from the Bishop Rock lighthouse, and by the time the rescue boats arrived two of her lifeboats had been smashed when the funnel collapsed on them, two had jammed, and only two managed to get away with the few passengers and crew who had survived the heavy seas. Over 300 lives were lost, just 37 were saved. John Gibson prepared the newspaper reports of the wreck, and for several days and nights Alexander transmitted them to the ship's owners, the relatives of the passengers and the world at large until he collapsed exhausted. Over fifty years later *The Scillonian* magazine carried an account of the incident as recalled by Alexander at the age of 75, when he was described as being 'exceptionally active for his years' and possessing a 'marvellous memory'.

ONE OF THE SEVERAL GIBSON ADVERTISEMENTS IN THEIR OWN GUIDE TO THE SCILLY ISLES.

The sudden call on the powers of the little village office was unprecedented, and cannot be adequately described. It was a fearful rush like an overwhelming avalanche; the office, which was in the shop, was crammed to suffocation, messages poured in over the counter and in less than an hour all the regular official forms were used up, and from then on messages were written on any and every kind of substance: wrapping paper, old envelopes, scraps of every colour and mostly written with pencil, making them doubly hard to read, especially German, which anyone who has ever tried to decipher it will understand.

Most of the passengers were wealthy American and German people and messages to those countries cost over 2s per word, many of them running into pounds each with minute descriptions of bodies of the drowned, and a great heap of material for despatch piled up faster than it was possible to clear. . . all the members of Mr Gibson's household were pressed into service, but Mr Alexander, being the only expert telegraphist, had to bear the burden of the actual operating with obsolete instruments which should have been in a museum.

By the light of a paraffin lamp the work would steadily go on until the dawn of another day; wet cloths were constantly applied to his [Alexander's] head to keep him awake, the eyes became so utterly tired out and strained that the words all ran together: his father stood by him . . . while the sending arm became numb and senseless and was supported by a bandage around the neck. . . These severe conditions lasted nearly a fortnight, when one midnight he suddenly collapsed and passed into a state of complete unconsciousness from which he did not awake for over thirty hours.

Afterwards the three Gibsons set about photographing the aftermath: a lifeboat fetched up on Town Beach, St. Mary's; the mass graves and burial of the victims (Plate 28); and later, a still-life picture of one of the salvaged United States $20 gold pieces (Plate 29). The ship carried immense treasure, 300,000 dollars in gold coin, most of it brought up by divers.

By 1879, John had given up his studio at the Promenade in Penzance. He secured a lease of a substantial property in 10 Market Jew Street, took both his sons into the business, retitled it Gibson & Sons, and with a showman's flourish opened the new shop, named the Mount's Bay Studio. He made sure no one could ignore it. The Gibsons' name was on the outside of every one of the five floors. The Union Jack flew from the fourth floor balcony, and the ground floor windows were covered with Gibson photographs. The portrait studio was equipped with the latest lighting gear. The Census for 1881 lists John, Alexander and Herbert as occupying 10 Market Jew Street, with John's four daughters, Emily, Margaret, Clara and Annie. Emily and Margaret are described as shop assistants, Clara and Annie as scholars. It appears that almost the whole family of working age was employed in the business.

The three photographer Gibsons continued to increase their already large archive of photographs of every aspect of Cornwall and Scilly: people, views, shipwrecks, archaeological relics, sacred and mystical sites, churches, industry – the list is endless. In the Penzance studio there were 2,000 pictures, arranged in albums for viewing and offered for sale to the public. The Gibsons were privately commissioned to photograph people and buildings, supplied photographs for the *Illustrated London News*, and later for other papers, and took wreck photographs for insurers and official inquiries. They took on the competition with a vengeance, and in 1884 John bought the freehold of the building which extended through to Bread Street, increasing the depth of the combined shop and studio to about 100 feet. The premises were then described as an exceptionally large studio, with 'every advantage which excellent lighting and a very complete set of modern photographic apparatus can give it'. The catalogued collection of 2,000 pictures was said to include 'a wonderful variety of subjects, many of them treated with exceptional skill by Mr Alexander Gibson who exhibits no small merit as a painter, and is certainly an art photographer'. They sold a series of postcards, then fashionable, of scenic views and shipwrecks. In fact they were

DING DONG MINE WORKINGS, PHOTOGRAPHED BY ALEXANDER GIBSON C.1880.
HE WAS LATER TO THROW A LARGE NUMBER OF HIS CORNISH PLATES DOWN A MINESHAFT HERE.

photo-cards, as each one was made from a plate – labour-intensive but producing finer images than the later mass-produced, machine-made copies.

The Gibsons' interest in technology is best illustrated in the large collection of photographs of the flower industry of Scilly. Although only a few are included in this book, they took photographs showing every aspect of the techniques of cultivation, as well as the picking, packing and transportation to market. The flower industry was at its height in the 1890s, with hundreds of new varieties being added every year, mainly from bulbs imported from Holland. The growers advertised over a hundred different varieties of narcissi alone. There can be few sights lovelier than the flower fields of Scilly in full bloom in early spring. This group of photographs (of which Plates 76-82 are a selection) will be of great interest to students of the evolution of modern horticulture.

These years at the end of the century were the most productive for the three Gibsons. Both the Mount's Bay Studio in Penzance and the Clarence House premises in Church Street, now renamed the Lyonesse Studio, flourished. The brothers both spent time in Scilly. Alexander took tourist photographs during the summer season, whilst both brothers chased the inevitable shipwrecks, increasing the collection which was later to be published in a series of cards and photographs that sold all over the world.

Alexander had by then become a recognised local eccentric. Tall and bearded with a long stride and longer hair, he wore a velvet cap and would regularly stop in the street to gossip to the locals. He had become an acknowledged antiquarian, with a keen interest in archaeology and ancient legends, subjects that both Scilly and West Cornwall were noted for. 'The place is pre-eminently the region of dream and mystery', wrote Thomas Hardy in 1870 about Cornwall. The standing stones which pepper the peninsular captivated Alexander, as did the remarkable feats of Bronze Age engineers in transporting and erecting the granite blocks, and he photographed them (Plates 70 and 71) without including his usual onlookers. A writer in *The Scillonian* magazine in 1934 describes Alexander in flowery terms: 'Endowed by nature with a poetic and highly romantic temperament, an active mentality and an insatiable craving for knowledge carried him far afield through the pathways of literature, while a critical observation of places, customs and people yielded such a rich harvest that he seems equally at home on any topic. He has been a keen and life-long student of pre-historic matters, an antiquarian of wide experience, and was many years ago appointed by the Director General of the Ordnance Survey Office their representative for the department of Archaeology in the Isles of Scilly.' For some time Alexander and Herbert collected relics and archaeological artefacts for the private museum they were to open in the Lyonesse Studio in Scilly.

Herbert was less flamboyant. He looked and dressed like a bank manager, but in later life he too could recount thrilling tales of smuggling and of the shipwrecks he had photographed. Solid and reliable, he was overshadowed by his dynamic brother; but if Alexander's graveside eulogy is to be believed, Herbert was far from being dull. Alexander recalled how close they were, in life as in work: 'When . . . I lay at the point of death with typhoid he watched by me unceasingly, and when given up by the doctors saved my life; in his intense yearning to keep me he would hold my feeble hands as would a mother, and then some mysterious power, a personal magnetism, flowed from him to me carrying some of his strength, and it was that and that only which kept me from "Crossing the Bar".'

As the century turned, John became less and less involved in the business. He was in his seventies, had never remarried, and now lived in the house alongside the studio in Church Street. Alexander and Herbert were effectively running the business and in 1910 they acquired his interest. John retired to the handsome village of St. Buryan, not far from Land's End, where he died in 1920.

By now a new Gibson had entered the scene. James, Alexander's son, born in 1901, joined the business as soon as he left school in 1916 and looked after the shop, whilst the brothers continued to work the summer season in Scilly and winter in Penzance. In 1925, however, Herbert and Alexander decided to part, perhaps because James now seemed the natural successor to Alexander, then 59. The Penzance end of the business was effectively run down. Mount's Bay Studio was closed, and Herbert moved to a shop and living premises at 34 Tolver Road in Penzance. There he carried on business as Gibson & Sons, offering 'Photographs of West Cornwall,

Pre-historic remains of great value to all Antiquarians, Churches, Old Stocks, Holywells, Manor Houses and other quaint subjects', as well as 'Shipwrecks on Cornish Coasts, a spectacular collection of world-wide fame, Wonderful Coast Scenery, Mining Scenes etc.' Alexander, now operating from the Lyonesse Studio, also as Gibson & Sons, produced the *Gibson Guide to the Scilly Isles* and gave his brother advertising space in it, though sadly tucked away in the end section between the chemists and the Cornish Cream restaurant. He also opened yet another new shop in St. Mary's near the Post Office, which, he announced, 'is never closed'.

James was a hard-working, humourless and not overly tolerant young man. He had entered a workplace of pioneers who were ageing and clinging on to ownership and control. His father never stopped moving, and probably talked continuously with a voice that had been likened to a 'clacking gull'. James had married at the age of 26, by which time he had worked in the business for over a decade. Trouble was brewing.

Alexander, after over fifty years running the business, was losing interest in the humdrum life of a shopkeeper, but not in archaeology, folklore and Druidism. James constantly complained that his father spent all his time 'yapping' about archaeology instead of watching the shop – and the pennies. The two men quarrelled bitterly. Alexander kept James on a low wage, and it seemed there was no future for him. Herbert, back from Penzance and living in Church Street, also could not get on with James. Alexander was frequently away in Penzance, and James, never a good communicator, was unable to persuade him that he should pay more attention to the Scilly business.

Separation was inevitable, but they could not even discuss terms. As a final insult, James opened a rival studio at Poltair, a few yards away from the Lyonesse studio. There was no room for two photographers in Scilly, let alone two egotists, intolerant of each other.

James carried on under his own name. The families did not speak as the animosity spread to Herbert and his family. Frank Gibson, James's son, who was just six at the time of the split, recalls that he sometimes peeped in the house to see his grandmother, never spoke to his grandfather, Alexander, and cannot remember ever meeting Herbert, who died in St. Mary's in 1937. An agreement was finally and grudgingly thrashed out between the now alienated father and son. For a sum, James was to get the bulk of the business. He already had all the archaeological plates of Cornwall, and all the Scilly photographs, and Alexander agreed to pass over the shipwreck plates which were in Penzance, probably stored, after the closure of the Mount's Bay Studios at Herbert's shop in Tolver Road. Alexander delivered them poorly packed to a Penzance carrier, where they were put aboard the steamer *Scillonian*, reaching Scilly miraculously undamaged. Alexander, so the story goes, was still consumed with fury. He took the remaining plates, of portraits, groups of people and scenic views, carted them to the disused Ding Dong tin mine at Gulval, and in what has been described as a Lear-like rage threw them down a thousand-foot shaft. Seventy years of dedicated work was destroyed.

Now James began to rebuild the business in his style. If John was the originator, Alexander and Herbert the creative lights, James was the craftsman. If he had been asked whether he thought photography was an art rather than a craft or a livelihood, James would probably have laughed at the question. Outwardly, he was a jobbing photographer: weddings, funerals, family portraits, and pictures for the newspapers when there was a good story. Eclipsed by the dazzling early talents of his forebears, he was known to stand for no artistic nonsense. Not surprisingly perhaps, that is how many saw him, and his contribution to the chronicle of the Gibson dynasty has either been understated or ignored. Yet the facts show that James was the most qualified of the family, an Associate of the Royal Photographic Society who quietly submitted his photographs to competitions and exhibitions all over the world. In 1933 and 1934, *The British Journal of Photography* almanac awarded him a medal for two pictures, 'Grey Seal' and 'Neptune's Splendour', and a French medal followed. In 1938 his seascape 'A Southerly Gale' won an award from the American Annual of Photography as 'a beautiful rare picture'. James also won medals from the Royal Photographic Society and the Irish Salon of Photography. All this occurred at the height of his battle with Alexander. The many hundreds of photographs he took represent a comprehensive record over two decades of events in the locality.

FRANK GIBSON PHOTOGRAPHED THE TANKER *TORREY CANYON*, WRECKED ON THE SEVEN STONES IN 1967.

James had inherited the family talent for adventurous journalism. Few accounts survive, either written down or in the family tradition, of the way in which the Gibsons went about getting their most dramatic shots from cliff edges or high vantage points in wild weather. Frank Gibson, James's son, and the present proprietor of the Gibsons' Scilly photographic business, remembers one series of pictures taken by his father in January 1947 of the rescue of a BBC reporter from three weeks' incarceration on the Bishop Rock lighthouse in stormy weather (Plates 88 and 89). In those days, small-plane flying was often dangerous. To get the photograph of Edward (later Viscount) Ward being taken off the Bishop by breeches buoy, the small single-engine plane had to hover at near stalling speed while James snapped the picture. Frank Gibson, at 16 now learning the business, sat in the back seat. Ward, who had been a prisoner of war of the Germans for three years, was on his first important radio assignment. The BBC had asked him to do the traditional Christmas Day broadcast in 1946, instead of their usual broadcaster, Wynford Vaughan Thomas. Being trapped in the lighthouse was for Ward a reliving of his days in the camp, now again a prisoner in the tower. If his rescue must have come as a relief to him, it was a tremendous scoop for James.

Shortly after Herbert died in 1937, Alexander moved to Oswestry in Shropshire. His wife died a few years later. Alexander occupied himself with archaeology and photography, writing and publishing a book about the history of Whittington Castle, which he illustrated with his own photographs, and a guidebook to his local parish church. A year before he died, in 1943, he was elected a member of the select Bardic Circle of Cornwall. This must have pleased the romantic mystic in him, though it might not have squared with his devotion to scientific archaeology. The Grand Bard recorded that Alexander was honoured 'for the good work of discovery and recording the ancient things of the Islands and West Cornwall', and added: 'Had your brother lived you may take it that the recognition we gladly give to you would have included him also.' Alexander's Bardic name was *Tas an Enesow*, Father of the Islands, which is another way of saying 'Grand old man of Scillonia', as the local newspaper put it. Alexander died at 87, on Christmas Eve, 1944 at the home of his only daughter in Wem, Shropshire. He had been looked after by his two maiden sisters in Oswestry, where he is buried alongside his wife.

Francis (Frank) Gibson, James's eldest son, was born in 1929, and joined the business at 16 as soon as he left Launceston College. Although James had a reputation for meanness, Frank remembers with gratitude his father paying to send him to college because his younger brother had won the only free scholarship for that year. Nevertheless, the classical tussle between father and son was about to be played out again. This time, however, Frank recognised their basic incompatibility, and after working for James for a few years and learning the elements of the photographic business, he tactfully left and in 1950 moved to mid-Cornwall. In St. Austell he joined Tom Corin, a local photographer, and learnt more about the trade and the new technology. The latter was a bone of contention between Frank and James. Frank felt that his father had fallen behind the times, using glass half and quarter plates when Frank had moved on to 2¼-inch film and the lighter cameras required for that format.

In St. Austell, Frank married a Cornish girl, Marie Boxer, born and bred near the famous China clay pits and a fellow employee in Tom Corin's processing laboratory. In 1957, with his family, he returned to Scilly and once again tried to work with his father in the business. But Frank had firm ideas about the future of the undertaking, and James was not one to cope with another strong mind. The 'partnership' lasted just two seasons, after which James, perhaps wearily, decided to retire. In 1958, he sold the business to Frank.

Under Frank's stewardship the business expanded. He built up the postcard, books and fancy goods side to supplement the income from photography and opened another shop in Hugh Town, though he continued the Lyonesse Studio in Church Street. Scilly was always in the news. There were shipwrecks as ever, and the *Torrey Canyon* oil spill disaster. There was also a local political interest, with Prime Minister Harold Wilson regularly staying at his holiday cottage on St. Mary's. Great treasure ships were being discovered by divers, the islands got the first scheduled helicopter service in Britain, and there were round-the-world sailors and rowers. Frank photographed all the events, ready to travel anywhere to catch a moment in many of his pictures that took them beyond the ordinary. Richard Branson must be one of the most photographed tycoons in the world, but Frank, with the Gibson flair for composition, has caught him charmingly with his young daughter Holly and a glass of

MARY WEARNE, PHOTOGRAPHED BY ALEXANDER GIBSON
ON NEWLYN BEACH,
C. 1885 (DETAIL OF PLATE 105).

obviously chilled white wine, in a beautifully balanced statement of 'Daddy's safe' and 'I'm back' (Plate 100). And there is nothing left out in the holiday snap (Plate 99) of Harold Wilson: populist Prime Minister, knapsack, vacuum flask, bare knees, and genuine family pleasure.

Like his grandfather, Frank appreciates that photographs should be seen by later generations – and that there is a demand for looking at the people, places and events of the past, for pleasure, nostalgia and understanding. He has collected and published groups of Gibson photographs spanning the decades.

Frank is also a shrewd businessman. Like most of the Gibsons, he saw the economic need to practise commercial photography, but like them too he believes that photography is also an art, an expression of mood and colour, not just a literal representation. His seascape (Plate 2) has a sense of light and movement that evokes Turner. The Gibson link with painting is best seen in Plates 47, 48 and 105, coastal scenes photographed during the most prolific period of the Newlyn School of painters.

It is thought that some of the school used Gibson photographs to complete and enhance their paintings. Look at Stanhope Forbes's ambitious and famous studies, *Newlyn Slip* and *Fish Sale on a Cornish Beach*, painted in the 1880s. In plate 105, Alexander portrays Mary Wearne, later to become Forbes's model in *The Hopeless Dawn* and *The Last Rites*.

I have known Frank for over thirty years. To describe him as modest and guarded would be to conceal his awareness of the value of his work and that of his ancestors. My acceptance of his reticence to talk about his ideas of photography, and his family history, comes from an understanding that underlies the basis of our friendship. Not until I embarked on this book did I discover how little I really knew, and how hard I would have to work to prise out the information I needed to flesh out the later Gibson family history. Frank is the custodian of a rare storehouse of information and images dating from the earliest days of photography to the present – a present that will also soon become the past.

Twenty years ago, in a BBC film about the Gibson shipwreck photographs, Frank lamented the end of the Gibson line. 'I have three daughters, no sons,' he announced ruefully. Maybe he had forgotten that Marie, his wife, had also worked in a photographic studio. Frank has now 'retired', but he is still to be seen with his camera, waiting for the right shaft of light or swell of the sea.

As recently as June 1996 he was there to record a visit to Scilly by the Prince of Wales, just as over ninety years ago the Gibsons photographed another Prince of Wales at the opening of the Marconi station in Poldhu (see Plate 96).

Meanwhile Frank's youngest daughter, Sandra Kyne, has returned to Scilly from Devon, and is working as her father's assistant and student. When Frank is not available, Sandra is there. The remarkable Gibson succession continues, and Sandra has a son. . .

THE PRINCE OF WALES,
PHOTOGRAPHED BY FRANK GIBSON IN SCILLY,
JUNE 1996.

THE GIBSON FAMILY

JOHN GIBSON
(1827–1920)

ALEXANDER
(1857–1944)

HERBERT
(1861–1937)

JAMES
(1901–1985)

FRANK
(1929–)

SANDRA
(1963–)

CHRONOLOGY OF THE GIBSON FAMILY

1811 James Gibson born St. Martins, Isles of Scilly, probably the son of John Gibson of St. Martins. Married Catherine Nance of St. Martins.

1827 John (son of James), the first Gibson photographer, born Aran Isles, Ireland.

1840 James Gibson, coastguard, died of rupture after pulling up a boat from the water. Buried near Cashell, Ireland.

1851 The census of this year records Catherine Gibson living at Higher Town, St. Martins.

1855 Marriage of John (described as a seaman, aged 28) to Sarah Gendall (aged 22) of St. Mary's, Isles of Scilly. Sarah's father Robert was born in Penzance.

1857 Alexander Gibson born.

1861 Herbert John Gibson born.

1864 Five Gibson children, including Herbert and Alexander, baptised at St. Mary's.

1869 Catherine, widow of coastguard James, buried at St. Mary's, aged 81.

1870 John made local correspondent for West Country Newspapers.

1871 Census for this year lists John, described as a grocer aged 43, as the family head in Porthcressa Street, St. Mary's; Sarah aged 38, his wife, born at St. Mary's; and the children: Emily (14, 'scholar'), Alexander (13, telegraph messenger), Margaret (11, 'scholar'), Herbert (9, 'scholar'), Clara, (4, 'scholar'), Annie (3). All the children were born in St. Mary's, as was Elizabeth Gendall, sister-in-law of John, described as a shop assistant (in Gibson's store).

1871 October 17. Sarah Gibson, wife of John Gibson, buried in Old Town churchyard, St. Mary's.

1873 The Post Office directory for this year lists John Gibson, grocer and tea dealer, at Porthcressa Street, St. Mary's.

1878 Kelly's Directory lists John Gibson, grocer and draper, Porthcressa St. and Bank St.

1881 Census: John Gibson, family head of 10 Market Jew Street, photographer and fancy goods dealer (this is the first confirmation of their trading title); Emily (24, shop assistant), Alexander (23, photographer), Margaret (21, shop assistant), Herbert (19, photographer), Clara (14, scholar), Annie Jane (13, scholar), Elizabeth Gendall, mother-in-law (74, assistant), Elizabeth Gendall, daughter of Elizabeth (44, unmarried dressmaker) ; she brought up the Gibson children after their mother's early death.

1883 Kelly's Directory lists John Gibson, of Richmond House, St. Clare Street, Penzance (private address); 10 Market Jew Street (trade address), photographer and fancy goods.

1893 All Gibsons in business at 10 Market Jew Street but now trading as Gibson & Sons.

1896 Herbert marries Rebecca, sister of Abigail Jenkins, and moves to Tolver Road, Penzance.

1901 James born in Penzance.

1902 Gibson & Sons also in business at Church Street, St. Mary's. Alexander's home address recorded as 15 Tolver Place, Penzance.

1910 John retires from the businesses and moves to St. Buryan, Cornwall.

1920 John dies and is buried in St. Buryan.

1929 Frank born in St. Mary's.

1937 Herbert dies in St. Mary's where he is buried. Alexander commutes to Scilly from Penzance.

1939 James carries on business in Church St., St. Mary's in competition with his father. Later, Alexander sells to James after family rows. Alexander moves to Oswestry, Shropshire, his wife Abigail having predeceased him.

1944 Alexander dies in Oswestry.

1958 Frank takes over the business from James.

1963 Frank's daughter Sandra born in St. Mary's.

1985 James, who has retired to Falmouth, dies and is buried in St. Mary's.

1993 Sandra carries on the business in St. Mary's.

THE
GIBSON
PHOTOGRAPHS

BEHOLD THE SEA

(OPPOSITE) 1. SEA DEFENCES BREACHED, DECEMBER 1989.
(ABOVE) 2. THE ROCKS OF SCILLY, MINEFIELDS FOR SHIPS.

3. The captain and mate of the schooner *Enterprise*, which foundered off Hayle in 1903.

4. PORTHCRESSA BEACH, SCILLY, WHERE GREAT SAILING SHIPS WERE BUILT, C. 1869.

(OPPOSITE) 5. THE *CITY OF CARDIFF*, BEACHED NEAR LAND'S END IN 1912.
(ABOVE) 6. 'ANOTHER ACT OF SPLENDID SERVICE': SENNEN LIFE-SAVING APPARATUS SAVED THE *CITY OF CARDIFF*'S CREW.

7. The wreck of the French nitrate clipper *Seine*, December 1900.

8. No 'bon voyage' for the passengers of the United States liner *Paris*, aground on 21 May 1899.

9. 'Valhalla' on Tresco, last resting place for the figureheads from shipwrecks.

10. Seaplane on Town Beach, St. Mary's, c. 1915.

(ABOVE) 11. A DIVER OFF LOOE IN 1912, ABOUT TO INVESTIGATE THE CENTURY-OLD WRECK OF THE WARSHIP *ANSON*.
(BELOW) 12. BOOTY FROM THE *ANSON*.

13. THE *SUFFOLK*, WHICH SANK OFF THE LIZARD IN 1886.

14. Dead cattle and cargo from the *Suffolk*.

15. Cotton bales at St. Mary's, salvaged from the *Brinkburn* in 1898.

(ABOVE) 16. If he missed a shipwreck, Alexander Gibson painted it and sold his photographs of the painting.
(BELOW) 17. Robin Knox-Johnston, on the penultimate day of his lone circumnavigation, in 1969.

18. THE DAY THE WHALES CAME IN, MOUNT'S BAY, 1 JULY 1911.

19. THE CHILEAN STEEL BARQUE *QUEEN MAB*, SALVAGED AND TOWED INTO ST. MARY'S IN OCTOBER 1903.

20. Dried Cornish pilchards loaded at Penzance, bound for Italy, c. 1885.
(OVERLEAF) 21. The WILLIAM CORY, which foundered off Cape Cornwall in 1910 with a cargo of pit props.

22. Retouched view of the horror of the *Minnehaha*, wrecked in 1874 with a cargo of guano.

23. TRAWLER FLEET IN MOUNT'S BAY, C. 1880.

(ABOVE) 24. The schooner SOCOA, after grounding at Cadgwith, 1906.
(BELOW) 25. A traditional Scilly 'gig', used for landing pilots, photographed in C. 1968.

26. The 'spirit' of the *Mildred*, Gurnard's Head, 1912.

SHIPWRECK
AND DEATH

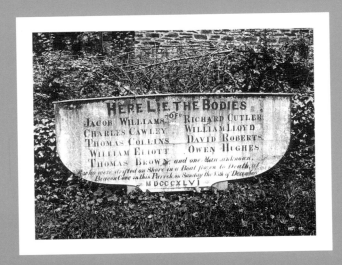

(OPPOSITE) 27. LAST RESTING PLACE OF TEN MEN FROM THE BARQUE *HOPE*, CAST ADRIFT IN 1846.
(ABOVE) 28. MASS GRAVES OF VICTIMS FROM THE *SCHILLER*, WRECKED IN 1875.

29. Gold coin, treasure from the *Schiller*.

(ABOVE) 30. THE 'GRAVE' OF ADMIRAL SIR CLOUDESELY SHOVELL, WASHED UP FROM THE *ASSOCIATION* IN 1707.
(INSET) 31. FIGUREHEAD FROM THE INDIA-BOUND SAILING SHIP *BENCOOLEN*, WHICH SANK IN 1862.

(ABOVE) 32. 'TWELVE SOULS HAD GONE TO ETERNITY . . .' IN THE *G. I. JONES*, WRECKED IN MOUNT'S BAY IN 1883.
(BELOW) 33. A FIGUREHEAD GUARDS THE GRAVES OF MEN FROM THE SWEDISH BRIGANTINE *WILLIAM*, WRECKED OFF BLACK ROCK IN 1894.

34. The view of the bodies from the *Mohegan*, wrecked off the Lizard in 1898, proved irresistible.

(ABOVE) 35. No shrouds on the faces of some of the dead from the *Mohegan* laid out in a church crypt.
(BELOW) 36. Mass grave for those lost on the *Mohegan*.

(ABOVE) 37. Tableau of death from the barque *Trifolium*, lost off Gwenver in 1914.
38. A figurehead in Morwenstow churchyard marks the graves of those lost on the brig *Caledonia*, wrecked off Sharpnose in 1842.

THE LAND,
THE COAST,
THE PLACES

(OPPOSITE) 39. THE FISHING FLEET AT ST. IVES.
(ABOVE) 40. SENNEN COVE, *C.* 1895. FISHING BOATS WERE HAULED UP TO THE ROUNDHOUSE.

65

(ABOVE) 41. SENNEN COVE, *C.* 1870. BEHIND THE COTTAGE WERE THE REMAINS OF AN ANCIENT CHAPEL.
(BELOW) 42. FIRST AND LAST HOTEL, NEAR LAND'S END, *C.* 1880.

43. NO WITCHES IN THE ROUNDHOUSE AT CROWS-AN-WRA, C. 1880.

44. The fishing fleet at Mousehole, c. 1890.

(ABOVE) 45. THE MOUSEHOLE HOME OF 'OLD DOLLY' PENTREATH, THE LAST CORNISH-LANGUAGE SPEAKER.
(BELOW) 46. THE OWNER OF THIS HOUSE IN MOUSEHOLE WAS KILLED BY A SPANISH CANNON BALL IN 1595.

(ABOVE AND OPPOSITE) 47/48. FISH SALE ON NEWLYN BEACH, C. 1884.

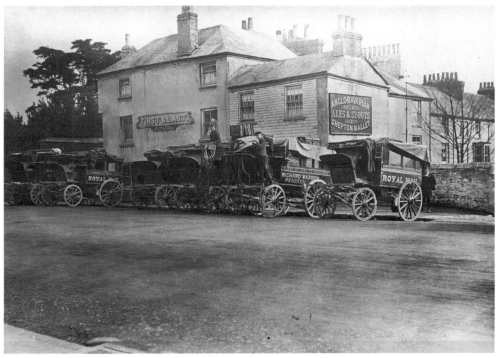

(ABOVE) 49: THE ICE STORE AT NEWLYN, C. 1880.
(BELOW) 50. STAGING POST TAVERN AT ALVERTON, NEAR PENZANCE, C. 1890.

51. WESTERN HOTEL, PENZANCE, C. 1900.

(ABOVE) 52. Penzance promenade was breached by a great storm in 1895.
(INSET) 53. A sailing ship unloads wood at Penzance, *c.* 1870.

54. Tax and the poor, Penzance, c. 1880.

(ABOVE) 55. THE KITCHEN OF A WEST PENWITH COTTAGE, 1880.
(BELOW) 56. LANGLEYS STORES IN MARKET JEW STREET, PENZANCE, c. 1890

57. Fishing cove at Porthgwarra, c. 1890. The caves lead to the houses above.

58. Coverack bay, *c.* 1900. Brandy was smuggled in here.

(*ABOVE*) 59. TOWN BEACH, ST. MARY'S, *C.* 1870.
(*BELOW*) 60. HUGH TOWN SCHOOL, ST. MARY'S, *C.* 1900.

61. Snow, a rarity in Scilly, blankets Hugh Town in 1891.

62. OLD TOWN CHURCH, SCILLY, AFTER THE BLIZZARD OF 1891.

(ABOVE) 63. Old Town, Scilly, in the 1880s. Only one of these houses survives.
(BELOW) 64. Kelp gathering, *c.* 1890.

65. THE CUTTER *BELLE* AND THE WRECK OF THE *JAMES ARMSTRONG* ON TOWN BEACH, ST. MARY'S, C. 1874.

HOLY PLACES
AND LEGENDS

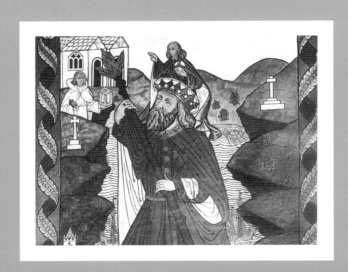

(OPPOSITE) 66. FIFTEENTH-CENTURY WALL PAINTING OF ST. CHRISTOPHER IN A CHURCH AT POUGHILL, *C.* 1880.
(ABOVE) 67. FIFTEENTH-CENTURY WALL PAINTINGS, REVEALED DURING THE 1890 RESTORATION OF THE CHURCH AT BREAGE.
(BELOW) 68. THE MERMAID OF ZENNOR IN THE CHURCH OF ST. SENARA.
(OVERLEAF) 69. GWENNAP PIT, NEAR REDRUTH, *C.* 1894. WESLEY PREACHED TO A HUGE CROWD HERE.

85

70. The Hurlers. According to legend, they were Sabbath-breakers turned to stone.

71. The twenty Druid stones of Boscawen-Un, *c.* 1890.

72. The dressing floor of the Consolidated Mines Company tin mine in St. Ives, 1885.

73. THE ENGINE HOUSES OF THE BOTALLACK MINE, C. 1890.

74. The Levant mine, one of the largest in Cornwall, now derelict.

75. THE UNITED MINE COMPANY'S TIN MINE NEAR ST. JUST, c. 1880.

FLOWERS

(OPPOSITE) 76. WILLIAM TREVELLICK, A SCILLY FLOWER INDUSTRY KING, AT ST. MARY'S, *c.* 1900.
(ABOVE) 77. AUGUSTUS SMITH, LORD PROPRIETOR OF
THE ISLES OF SCILLY AND 'FATHER OF THE FLOWER INDUSTRY', *c.* 1865.

78. William Trevellick and Mr E.N.V. Moyle check the hygrometer,
while a figurehead from a Scilly shipwreck keeps a weather eye.

79. BUNCHING FLOWERS, C. 1900.

80. THE PACKING HOUSE IN TRESCO ABBEY.

(ABOVE) 81. Loading the flowers for London at St. Mary's quay, *c.* 1910.
(BELOW) 82. Mr Craze, Mr Stevenson and Mr Thomas would be waiting for the Scilly flowers to arrive from Penzance.

'A STAR FOR SEAMEN'
LIGHTHOUSES

(OPPOSITE) 83. SUNDAY OUTING TO ROUND ISLAND LIGHTHOUSE, C. 1890.
(ABOVE) 84. THE BISHOP ROCK LIGHTHOUSE OFF SCILLY, 1887.
(BELOW) 85. THE WORKERS WHO BUILT BISHOP ROCK LIVED IN STORM-BATTERED
STONE HUTS ON THE BARREN ISLAND OF ROSEVEAR.
(OVERLEAF) 86. RELIEF OF THE BISHOP ROCK IN THE 1940S.

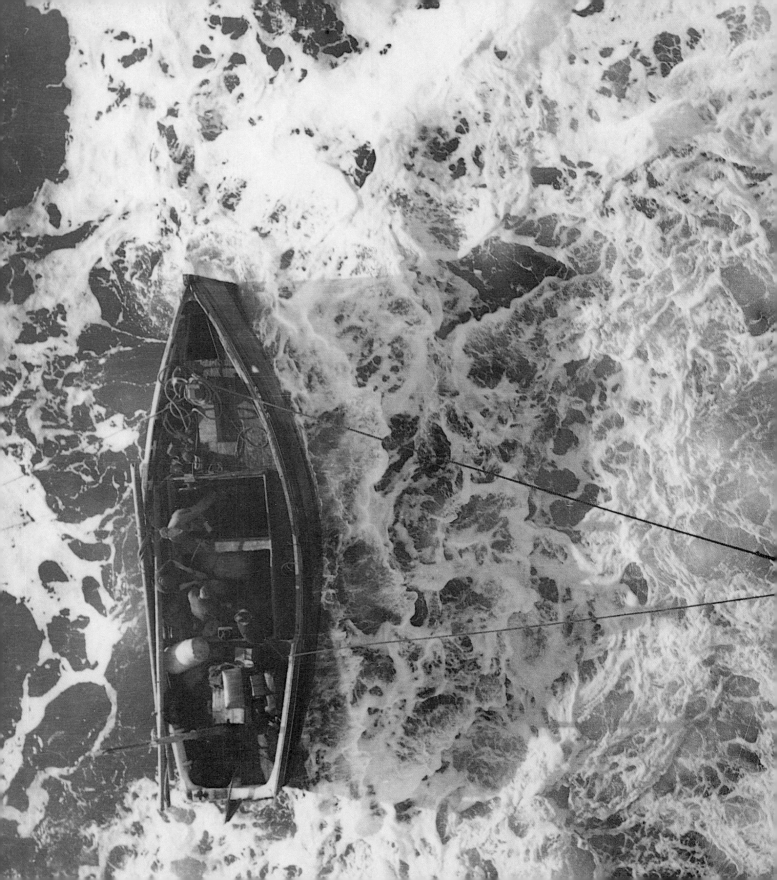

(ABOVE) 87. INTERIOR OF THE BISHOP ROCK LIGHTHOUSE, C. 1930.
(BELOW) 88. IN 1951, AFTER HIS CHRISTMAS DAY BROADCAST, EDWARD WARD WAS MAROONED FOR THREE WEEKS ON BISHOP ROCK.

(ABOVE) 89. EDWARD WARD (CENTRE) WITH RADIO ENGINEER STANLEY COOMBES AND THE LIFEBOAT CREW WHO GOT THEM OFF BISHOP ROCK.
(BELOW) 90. RELIEF BY HELICOPTER IN 1978. BISHOP ROCK IS NOW UNMANNED.

NEWS AND HAPPENINGS

(OPPOSITE) 91. The 'Fencibles', local volunteers in St. Mary's, C. 1870.
(ABOVE) 92. May Day in Hugh Town, Scilly, C. 1876.

(ABOVE) 93. Newlyn Fair, 1880.
(BELOW) 94. Opening of Penzance Dock, 10 November 1884.

95. Opening Day, Newlyn Pier, 3 July 1894.

(ABOVE) 96. The Prince and Princess of Wales with Marconi at the Marconi station in Poldhu, Cornwall, 1903.
(BELOW) 97. Auctioning the catch of a French crabber, caught poaching in territorial waters, St. Mary's, 1933.

98. The Queen Mother and the Lord Proprietor of the Islands in Tresco, 1962.

99. Happy holiday for Prime Minister Harold Wilson and family on Samson, Scilly, in 1965.

100. RICHARD BRANSON AND HIS DAUGHTER HOLLY AT ST. MARY'S IN 1985,
AFTER BEING RESCUED WHEN HIS BOAT *VIRGIN ATLANTIC* FOUNDERED.

IMAGES OF
PEOPLE

(OPPOSITE) 101. CRIME AND PUNISHMENT, CAMELFORD, C. 1900.
(ABOVE) 102. PENZANCE URCHINS, C. 1890.

(OPPOSITE) 103. 'NATIVE OF PENZANCE', C. 1890.
(ABOVE) 104. JOHN DIVANE OF PENZANCE, 'A HERO OF THE INDIAN MUTINY'.

(ABOVE) 105. FISHERWOMEN ON NEWLYN BEACH, C. 1885.
(INSET) 106. A CORNISH FISHWIFE OR 'JOUSTER', 1880.

(LEFT) 107. JACOB AND MRS DEASON OF ST. AGNES, SCILLY, C. 1895.
(RIGHT) 108. THE BILLINGSGATE MARKET FISH BUYER'S OFFICE AT NEWLYN, C. 1880.

(TOP LEFT) 109. FETCHING WATER, C. 1890.
(RIGHT) 110. BARNACLE-CLAD TIMBER BAULK, C. 1900.
(BOTTOM LEFT) 111. BAITING FISH HOOKS AT SENNEN COVE, C. 1895.

(TOP LEFT) 112. WESLEYAN METHODISTS, SCILLY, 1890.
(TOP RIGHT) 113. THE ALL-MALE NAUTILUS CLUB, A PENZANCE BOATING GROUP, *C.* 1900.
(BOTTOM LEFT) 114. THE SCILLONIAN WORKMEN WHO BUILT THE NEW QUAY AT PAR BEACH IN 1892.
(BOTTOM RIGHT) 115. DELUSIONS OF GRANDEUR: STATE BARGE ROWERS COSTUMED
BY LORD ST. LEVANS OF ST. MICHAEL'S MOUNT, *C.* 1890.

GIBSONS
IN CAMERA

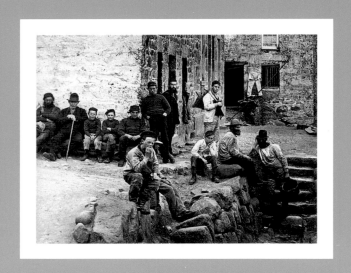

(OPPOSITE) 116. ALEXANDER GIBSON IN HIS OWN PHOTOGRAPH OF MOUSEHOLE FISHERMEN.
(ABOVE) 117. ARMORELS COTTAGE, SAMSON, SCILLY, C. 1890. JOHN GIBSON
IS IN THE FOREGROUND, HERBERT ON THE WALL.

(ABOVE) 118. Probably Alexander Gibson leaning, Herbert Gibson reclining,
photographed by John Gibson at Land's End, *c.* 1890.
(BELOW) 119. The old mine works at Gurnard's Head, *c.* 1870. The Gibsons'
cart for developing wet plates is in the foreground.

120. ALEXANDER (*LEFT*) AND JOHN GIBSON AT PIPER'S HOLE ON TRESCO, *C.* 1870.

(ABOVE) 121. ALEXANDER GIBSON (*MIDDLE, IN SUIT*) WITH FISHERMEN AT MOUSEHOLE, *C.* 1888.
(BELOW) 122. JOHN GIBSON AND THE STEAMER *ST. AUBIN*, STRANDED OFF THE LIZARD IN AUGUST 1902.

NOTES ON THE PHOTOGRAPHS

The photographs in this book have been reproduced from fine prints prepared from the original wet or dry glass plates, or photographic film. Where the original negative does not exist, fine prints have been made from the most contemporary prints that survive. Most of the illustrations of Cornwall have been made from such prints, as the original plates were destroyed when Alexander Gibson threw them down Ding Dong mine.

1/2. Frank Gibson.

3. The *Enterprize*, a wooden schooner from Beaumaris with a cargo of China clay, drifted helplessly about two miles from St. Ives Head, Cornwall on 11 September 1903, having lost all her canvas in a gale. Her crew of three men and a boy were rescued by the Hayle lifeboat after a dangerous sail to her aid. The cost of the lifeboat service was £18.12s.

Alexander Gibson, 1903.

4. Porthcressa beach in Scilly, where now children play, was once the place for the building of great sailing ships like the *David Auterson*, the last vessel built on the beach. Launched in 1871, she circumnavigated the world on her maiden voyage.

John Gibson, 1870.

5/6. The *City of Cardiff*, a steamer only six years old, was driven ashore on the Cornish coast near Land's End on 28 March 1912, and pounded to pieces in a heavy gale within a few hours. Her crew of twenty-seven were saved by the crew of the Sennen life-saving apparatus.

Alexander/Herbert Gibson, 1912.

7. 'Bravery and exciting scenes' provided the spectacle as the French iron barque *Seine* grounded in the sand at Perranporth in horrific weather on 28 December 1900. The crew were pulled through the boiling surf in exhausted condition as the rescue team succeeded in sending a rocket and line aboard.

Alexander/Herbert Gibson, 1900.

8. On 21 May 1899 the United States liner *Paris*, with a gross tonnage of 11,000, was the largest ship ever to have fetched up on the British coast, the end of the voyage for 756 passengers and crew.

Alexander/Herbert Gibson, 1899.

9. In 1840, Augustus Smith, the authoritarian Lord Proprietor of the Scilly Islands, founded 'Valhalla', the last resting place for many of the figureheads and carved decorations from ships that met their end on the Islands. It opened to the public in a verandah shaped like a grotto on the island of Tresco, where the conserved and repainted figureheads can be seen today.

Alexander Gibson, *c.* 1880.

10. Herbert Gibson.

11/12. The frigate HMS *Anson* (44 guns) sailed from Falmouth on Christmas Eve, 1807 for Black Rocks, as one of the guard ships of the Channel Fleet. Mistaking Land's End for the Lizard, the Captain did not realise his error until a look-out sighted 'breakers ahead', by which time the ship's fate was sealed. At a time 'when it was supposed the work of death had ceased', a Methodist preacher searching the wreck came across some survivors, including women, and led them to safety; criminals who had been confined in irons below also emerged. Almost 150 people died. For over a century, divers tried to salvage the valuable parts of the vessel and its contents. Captain Anderson and his 'hard-hat' divers recovered cannons and other objects, and Anderson dressed up in his Sunday best to be photographed with one of the cannons.

Alexander Gibson, 1912.

13/14. When the *Suffolk*, a steamer bound from Baltimore to London with a cargo of cattle, ran aground in a dense fog under the old Lizard Head on 28 September 1886, the terrified animals huddled at the fore of the vessel. A few were saved, most drowned. Some managed to make land at the foot of the cliffs, but as there was no means of getting them all up many were slaughtered on the spot. The Gibson cameras captured the scenes from the clifftop and the beach.

Herbert Gibson, 1886.

15. The lifeboat men on St. Mary's in Scilly were making merry at a party when they were called to the rescue as the steamer *Brinkburn* struck the Maiden Bower Rocks. The programme for the evening party was 'singing, music and games from seven to nine p.m. Then a cold collation of roast beef, ham cake and tea . . . but just after midnight as the merry dancers glided gracefully over the floor . . . a shout rang through the hall . . . A WRECK! A WRECK!' Both lives and cotton bales were saved.

Alexander Gibson, 1898.

17. Around the world in 314 days. On the 313th day, Frank Gibson went by boat to the Bishop Rock off Scilly to photograph Robin Knox-Johnston in *Suhaila*.

Frank Gibson, 1969.

18. To the shame of the community, some of the inhabitants at Mount's Bay cut fillets from the bodies of the live stranded whales.

Alexander Gibson, 1 July 1911.

19/20. Herbert Gibson.

21. Alexander Gibson.

22. The *Minnehaha*, a fully rigged sailing ship voyaging from the Guanape Isles to Falmouth and Dublin, struck the rocks at Peninnis Head, Scilly after a disagreement between the Captain ('Put the helm hard up!') and the Pilot ('Put the helm hard down!'). For that dispute the only passenger and ten of the nineteen crew lost their lives, whilst the survivors scrambled through the rigging as the ship broke up, and the Gibsons snapped the scene.

Alexander Gibson, 1874.

23/24. Alexander/Herbert Gibson.

25. Frank Gibson.

26. Alexander/Herbert Gibson.

27. The longboat from the Liverpool barque *Hope* drifted into Mawgan Porth, Cornwall on 12 December 1846 with ten sailors frozen to death and another six frost-bitten and exhausted. On the homeward journey from Rio they had abandoned the sinking ship off Fishguard Bay in a blinding snowstorm. The dead were buried in Mawnan churchyard with a replica of the stern of the longboat to mark their graves.

Alexander/Herbert Gibson, *c.* 1865.

28/29. The *Schiller*, a German liner with 284 passengers and 118 crew, left New York on 28 April 1875. Despite a prize of champagne for the first of her passengers or crew who heard the Bishop Rock foghorn or saw her light, she hit the treacherous rocks of the Retarrier Ledge off the Western Rocks in dense fog. No fewer than 239 passengers and 72 of the crew perished in the huge seas which swept over the stricken liner. She carried a treasure of $300,000 which was salvaged by divers over the years. Rock had to be blasted in Old Town churchyard to make way for the mass graves of 147 of the drowned victims.

Alexander Gibson, *c.* 1890.

30. Of the many myths about the tragic loss of Admiral Cloudesley Shovell, his flagship the *Association*, three more of his warships and almost 2,000 men on 22 October 1707, this place on Porth Hellick, Scilly – supposed to have been where he landed alive, was robbed of his ring, died and was temporarily buried – is the most spurious. The stage-set 'grave' is the likely spot where his drowned body was fetched up after the disaster.

Alexander Gibson, *c.* 1890.

31. A large, fully rigged wooden East Indiaman, the *Bencoolen* left Liverpool for Bombay with a crew of thirty-one men and a boy. With bad discipline and some of the crew drunk, she lost her masts in a gale and drifted onto the shore at Bude Haven. Twenty-four of the crew died, and a subsequent inquiry left many questions unanswered, after conflicting allegations and counter-allegations. Thirteen of the drowned seamen were buried under the watchful eye of the figurehead in Bude Haven church.

Alexander/Herbert Gibson, *c.* 1865.

32. Only two of the thirteen crew of the *G. I. Jones*, a barque bound from Bull River, Canada to Falmouth with a cargo of phosphate, survived when she hit the rocks at Cuddan Point in Mount's Bay, Cornwall on 1 September 1883. Despite the Falmouth pilot being aboard, the ship failed to weather the seas off the Lizard. Up to his neck in the water, the pilot was heard to cry: 'God help me, I am done for now.' The coroner and undertaker came to view the bodies washed up on the shore.

Herbert Gibson, *c.* 1883.

33. Alexander/Herbert Gibson.

34/35/36. When the liner *Mohegan*, sailing from London to New York, hit the beetling chain of submerged rocks known as the Manacles off Falmouth on 14 October 1898, the weather was fair and clear. No deck officer survived to explain the disaster. The only warning sign of the submerged reef, a notorious trap for mariners, was a solitary tolling buoy. 'Years has this warning voice sounded over the restless deep, many times has its message of mercy been turned into the death knell of scores of hapless men, women and children as they struggled and fought for life where mercy has no ear.' Amidst heart-rending scenes of panic and terror, heroism and death, the deadly Manacles took their biggest toll. Sixty-two of the crew of 100 and 44 of the 57 passengers died, and the Gibsons' cameras chronicled it all.

Alexander/Herbert Gibson, 1894.

37. Alexander/Herbert Gibson.

38. The Reverend Robert Stephen Hawker, High Churchman, poet and exhibitionist, served the parish of Morwenstow, and campaigned to save the soul of shipwrecked sailors by burying them in consecrated ground. The dead from the *Caledonia* were among his successes.

Gibson, *c.* 1865.

39. Alexander/Herbert Gibson.

40. The fishing boats were hauled up by a man capstan. In the building on the right of the photograph, pilchards were pressed into barrels.

Gibson, *c.* 1895.

41. The ancient holy house, known as Chapel Idne, is thought to date from the eleventh century.

Gibson, *c.* 1870.

42. John Gibson.

43. With no north side of dark corners in which to hide, the roundhouses of Cornwall were built to thwart the Devil. At Crows-an-Wra (the Witches' Cross) the roundhouse sold snuff and tobacco.

Alexander Gibson, *c.* 1880.

44. Mousehole, said to be a corruption of the Cornish word 'mouzel', has been a port and then a fishing village since 1392, and is still 'un-reformed by artists and unspoiled by vandals'.

Alexander Gibson, *c.* 1890.

47/48. Newlyn, still famed as a centre for artists, provided the images for several of the Newlyn School. Stanhope Forbes, who used local people as his models, is said to have used Gibson photographs to finish painting his famous canvas *A Fish Sale on the Beach*.

Alexander Gibson, *c.* 1884.

49. Alexander Gibson.

52. Alexander/Herbert Gibson.

56. Mr Langley was the first shopkeeper to expose his wares on the street in Penzance. There was so much pilferage that he was forced to place wire netting between the hungry hands and the fruit. The photographer posed Jan Saint Ives, a lively local character who delivered goods on his barrow, in the forefront of the photograph.

Gibson, *c.* 1890.

58. In his first report of the century, the local Customs Officer wearily noted that in the previous year, 'in spite of the utmost vigilance, no fewer than 7,000 ankers of brandy had been successfully run ashore in Coverack Bay.'

Gibson, *c.* 1900.

60. For this posed picture, not every child 'watched the birdie'.

Alexander Gibson, *c.* 1890.

61/62. Alexander Gibson.

64. Alexander Gibson.

66. St. Christopher (replete with seductive mermaid) in what was probably a cruciform church with thirteenth-century remains at Poughill. There are two large St. Christophers reputedly repainted by Frank Salisbury.

Alexander Gibson, c. 1880.

67. The wall paintings of St. Christopher and Christ of the Trades had been whitewashed after the Reformation. Alexander Gibson immediately recorded them when the church was restored.

Alexander Gibson, 1890.

68. Young Matthew Trewhella sang, with a fine voice, in the village and the church at Zennor. Lured away to a nearby stream which runs down to the sea by a beautiful woman, a stranger, who sat in the back of the church, he was never seen again. Local legend says she was a mermaid, unlucky to sailors, and that on a warm summer evening the young lovers can be heard singing beneath the sea. Carved in wood at the end of a pew in the fifteenth-century village church of St. Senara, the siren Mermaid of Zennor beckons.

Alexander Gibson, 1890.

69. 'And I shall scarce see a larger congregation till we meet in the air', was how John Wesley commented on the 30,000 worshippers (his estimate) at Gwennap Pit near Redruth. He exhorted them to holiness, and a look at some of the large chapels on Cornwall is testament to the hold he had on the Cornish.

Alexander Gibson, c. 1890.

70. Alexander Gibson.

71. Difficult to count with the eye, these Druidical stones are the remains of three stone circles.

Alexander Gibson, c. 1890.

73. Perched like sentinels at the margins of the sea, the engine houses of the Botallack mine, a rich source of tin and copper since 1721, are now ruins of industrial archaeology. The galleries of the mine run beneath the sea for over a third of a mile from the shore. Alexander Gibson caught the engine houses just before they became a lonely emblem of the past. The great days of mining were almost over, companies went bankrupt, and miners emigrated *en masse*.

Alexander Gibson, c. 1890.

76/78/79/80/81/82. In 1867 William Trevellick packed some narcissi into a hat box and sent them to Covent Garden. He got a half crown for them, and the Scilly flower industry was born. The climate in Scilly favoured flower-growing in the open, so long as the beds could be sheltered from the prevailing winds. The industry developed, with the increase of varieties of narcissi from Dutch bulbs, and almost every man, woman and child was recruited during the picking and bunching season. The Gibsons recorded every detail of the trade.

Alexander/Herbert Gibson, 1885–1910.

77. Educated at Harrow and Oxford, Augustus Smith, a man of vision and robustness, attempted to reform and rehabilitate the poverty-stricken Isles of Scilly and its inhabitants. He was one of the two aspirants (with William Trevellick) to the title of the Father of the Flower Industry, as well as being the Lord Proprietor of the Islands, and ruled with not always benign autocracy.

John Gibson, 1865.

83. Seamen have always needed protection from the rocks that dot the Isles of Scilly like natural minefields. Round Island light was built in 1887, on a deserted islet. Outings to the Rock were the occasion for elegant Sunday best, and both men and women made it a regular tradition until a visitor was injured and sued Trinity House for compensation.

Alexander Gibson, c. 1890.

84/85. Bishop Rock lighthouse was first built in 1845 but the whole structure was destroyed in a gale in 1850. Rebuilt in 1852, it was recased and rebuilt again in the 1880s. The workmen lived in stone huts on the rocky, barren and uninhabited island of Rosevear far out amongst the Western Rocks of Scilly, holding parties to brighten the stark and isolated life on the tiny rock. The coloured lights and music could sometimes be seen and heard eight miles away on St. Mary's. James Douglass, the lighthouse builder and engineer, taught the men to live on limpets and puffins' eggs, and in the evenings would play his flute.

Herbert Gibson, c. 1887–90.

86. All the men, food, fuel and letters had to be ferried to the Bishop Rock by small boat. The seas breaking on the rock made the task hazardous, and both supplies and men had to be winched up to the first port of the light – the men by breeches buoy, a tricky and perilous procedure. The relief boat had to be kept steady using only its engine – and Captain Stee, shown in this photograph, was renowned for his skill and courage.

James Gibson, c. 1930.

87/88/89. James Gibson.

90. The last man left Bishop Rock in 1994. For some years the relief had been carried out by helicopter on a pad built on the top of the light. Now the Bishop, like virtually every other rock light, is deserted. The silicon chip reigns. Four centuries of lighthouse keepers are gone for ever.

Frank Gibson, 1978.

91. Alexander Gibson.

92. John Gibson.

94. A jubilant crowd greeted the opening of the new Penzance floating dock in 1884. It opened up the prospects of extending the conveyance of goods between Penzance, London and other centres, avoiding the shortcomings of the tidal harbour to enable grain vessels to discharge their cargoes.

Gibson, 1884.

95. Newlyn was in its heyday on 3 July 1894 when with brass bands, flags and triumphal arches the North Pier was opened. Not only was the fishing industry flourishing, but Penlee stone, quarried on the coast, was used in the construction of Waterloo Bridge and the Bank of England in London.

Gibson, 1894.

97. James Gibson.

98. Frank Gibson.

99. Harold and Mary Wilson loved the Scillies, where they had a holiday home. They moved freely and were well liked. In 1965, then Prime Minister, Harold Wilson gave a press conference on the deserted island of Samson. His modest grave at Old Town Church in St. Mary's is amongst commoners, his friends and neighbours, as he would have wished.

100. Frank Gibson.

Frank Gibson, 1965.

103. Alexander Gibson.

104. 'Come on boys, it is death or glory.' Private John Divane, of the 1st Battalion Kings Royal Rifle Corps, won the Victoria Cross storming the Cashmere Gate, at Delhi, during the Indian Mutiny in September 1857. Hearing that call to duty, his fellow soldiers yelled, 'You go on, Johnny, and we will follow.' Divane was wounded and lost a leg. When he came to in the army hospital he said, 'Never mind, John Divane, here's a shilling a day for life.' He spent his last years wearing his medal, and a wooden leg, and hawking fish, dying at the age of 65 and leaving a widow and several children unprovided for. He died in Penzance, and was buried in an unmarked grave until in 1993 the army paid for a proper headstone to be erected.

Gibson, 1880.

107. Alexander Gibson.

112. John Gibson.

117. Augustus Smith depopulated Samson, one of the Isles of Scilly, in 1842 – he toyed with the idea of turning it into a deer park or ostrich farm. Sir Walter Besant visited Scilly in 1884 and wrote his sentimental novel *Armorel of Lyonesse* about Samson. This ruined cottage bore the name of his heroine, Armorel, and visitors would flock to it.

Alexander Gibson, 1890.

120. Piper's Hole on Tresco, Scilly, is a cavern at the centre of which is a small lake. An intrepid explorer can cross the lake to the other side where a sandy beach stretches to the end of the cavern. The cave inspired a legend of romance during the battle for the surrender of the Scillies in the civil war, when in 1651 Admiral Blake's troops fought their way across the island.

Herbert Gibson, 1870.

Topical as ever: Tony Blair at Lord Wilson's funeral in Scilly, photographed by Sandra (Gibson) Kyne.

BIBLIOGRAPHY

Arlott, John, Cowan, Rex, and Gibson, Frank. *Island Camera: The Isles of Scilly in the Photography of the Gibson Family* (David & Charles, 1972)

Cowan, Rex. *Castaway and Wrecked* (Duckworth, 1978)

Cowan, Zélide Teague. *The Story of Samson, An Island Community of Scilly* (Englang Publishing, 1991)

Fowles, John. *Shipwreck. Photography by the Gibsons of Scilly* (Cape, 1974)

Gibson, Frank. *A Maritime Album* (Gibson, n.d.)

Gibson, Frank. *The Savage Sea* (Gibson, n.d.)

Gibson, Frank. *The Isles of Scilly: Eye Witness, 1958-1984* (Gibson, n.d.)

Gibson, Frank. *The Isles of Scilly: Eye Witness. A Continuation 1985-1990* (Gibson, n.d.)

Gibson, Frank. *My Scillonian Home: its past, its present, its future* (Gibson, n.d.)

Grigson, Geoffrey. *The Scilly Isles* (Paul Elek, 1948).

Larn, Richard and Bridget. *Shipwreck Index of the British Isles. Volume One: Isles of Scilly and Cornwall* (Lloyd's, 1995).

Mumford, Clive. *Portrait of the Isles of Scilly* (1967)

Noall, Cyril (and Douglas Williams). *The Book of Penzance* (Barracuda Books, 1983).

Noall, Cyril. *The Illustrated Past: Penwith* (Barracuda Books, 1978)

Thomas, Charles. *Views and Likenesses. Photographers and Their Work in Cornwall and Scilly 1839-1870* (Royal Institution of Cornwall, 1988)